Abhidharmasamuccaya

Asanga's
Abhidharmasamuccaya
by Traleg Kyabgon

KTD Publications
Woodstock, New York

Published by KTD Publications
335 Meads Mountain Road
Woodstock, New York 12498

Abhidharmasamuccaya
by Traleg Kyabgon
These teachings were given by Traleg Kyabgon at E-Vam Buddhist Institute, Melbourne, 1983.

For further information please contact:
E-Vam Buddhist Institute
171 Water Street
Chatham, New York 12037
Tel: (518) 392-6900
www.evam.org

ISBN: 978-1-934608-47-0

© 2013 E-Vam Buddhist Institute. All rights reserved. No part of this book may be reproduced in any form or by any means without written permission from Traleg Kyabgon, except in the case of brief quotations embodied in critical articles and reviews.

Printed in the USA on PCR acid-free paper.

Contents

MIND

Evolution of Consciousness 3
Three Constitutive Principles of Reality 23
Yogacara Proofs for the Evolution of Consciousness 35
Five Skandhas 53
Relative and Absolute Truth 87
Four Factors of Basic Being 101

MENTAL EVENTS

Five Omnipresent Mental Events 113
Five Object-determining Mental Events 133
Eleven Healthy Mental Factors 143
Six Unhealthy Mental Factors 157

PATH AND FRUITION

The Five Paths 179

Traleg Kyabgon Rinpoche, E-Vam Institute, Chatham NY 2009

Traleg Kyabgon
A Short Biography

Traleg Kyabgon Rinpoche (1955–2012) was born in Eastern Tibet and recognized at the age of two by His Holiness the Sixteenth Gyalwang Karmapa—the head of the Karma Kagyu lineage—as the ninth incarnation of the Traleg tulkus. This lineage can be traced back to the time of Saltong Shogam, a contemporary of the first Karmapa. Traleg Rinpoche was enthroned as the Abbot of Thrangu Monastery in Tibet before being taken to safety in India following the Chinese invasion of his country. There he continued the rigorous training prescribed for tulkus born with responsibilities as major lineage holders in the Tibetan tradition of Vajrayana Buddhism. This training included five years of study at Sanskrit University in Varanasi and several years at Rumtek Monastery, the main seat of the Karma Kagyu Lineage. Not only did Traleg Rinpoche receive the complete teachings of the Karma Kagyu tradition of Vajrayana Buddhism, he also became well acquainted with the practices and philosophy of the Drugpa Kagyu strand of the Kagyu lineage after spending nine years studying with the Regent of the Drugpa Kagyu, the late Dungse Rinpoche, at his monastery in Darjeeling.

Traleg Rinpoche settled in Australia in 1980 to make the teachings and practices of the Kagyu tradition available there. He established Kagyu E-Vam Buddhist Institute in Melbourne in 1982, Maitripa Contemplative Center in

Healesville in 1997, Nyima Tashi in Auckland, New Zealand in 1999, and Yeshe Nyima in Sydney in 2008. Rinpoche traveled and taught in the United States from 1988 to 2010 and established E-Vam Buddhist Institute in Chatham, New York in 2003. Rinpoche also traveled widely in Europe, Canada, New Zealand, and Southeast Asia giving lectures and seminars on Buddhism and related topics.

Mind

Evolution of Consciousness

The *Abhidharmasamuccaya* belongs to the later development of Buddhism. Early Buddhism is known as Theravada or Hinayana and later Buddhism is known as the Mahayana. The Mahayana has two schools: the Madhyamaka (school of the middle way) and Yogacara (practitioners of yoga). Yoga in this case has very little to do with physical dexterity—how well you can twist your arms or fiddle your toes—and is very much related with learning how to meditate properly, how to relate to your own mind, and how to understand the mental states you go through during meditation. The *Abhidharmasamuccaya* presents that kind of overall structure in the fullest sense.

The founder of Yogacara was Asanga. As so often happens, it is very hard to really grasp or understand what Asanga was like as a person and what events really took place in his life because he lived roughly in the fifth century and historical facts seems to be somewhat secondary in this case. So many myths and legends revolve around a person who lived in such a remote age. Once we dispense with that we get to the *Abhidharmasamuccaya*. Asanga composed a lot of texts and among them the *Abhidharmasamuccaya* has a very prominent position. It is one of his most essential works and one of the most psychologically oriented works, which provides a framework as well as a general pattern, for how a practitioner should follow the path, develop him or herself, and finally attain buddhahood.

Rather than go into great detail about the *Abhidharmasamuccaya*—which might confuse rather than enlighten you—we are going to concern ourselves with basic concepts that will help you get the main points of Yogacara psychology or philosophy. Yogacara philosophy is not so much concerned with intellectual activities as it is with practice. At the same time, it gives some psychological explanations about how we function, how we exist, how we relate to the world, and so on.

Two of the most important notions related to the practice of Yogacara are *atman* and *dharma*. In this case, atman is not the Hindu notion of soul and dharma does not mean the Buddhist scriptures or Buddhism. In a Buddhist context, *dharma* normally means "the law." In a Hindu context, *dharma* means "the right way of living" or "right conduct" or something of that nature. How to treat your wife or your husband properly is dharma. But here whatever we experience is known as dharma. It could be an external object or it could be our own mental state. We experience pain, toothache, stomachache. That is all part of dharma. While anything that has to do with the subjective aspect of our life or experience is atman. We could say that dharma is objectivity and atman is subjectivity. We have these two situations.

Yogacara philosophy makes a bold statement, which is that both subjectivity and objectivity are transformations of consciousness. What we experience as well as the experiences themselves are transformations of our own consciousness, and there is nothing beyond that. There is no extra experiential thing for us to relate to. We will look at how this is possible. How does Yogacara try to explain this? What kinds of justifications do Yogacarin philosophers offer?

SUBSTRATUM OF AWARENESS

According to Yogacara, consciousness has three levels. The

first is known as the "substratum of awareness" (*alaya-vijnana* in Sanskrit). *Alaya* means "basic, basis, or substratum" and *vijnana* means "awareness" or "consciousness." Sometimes people translate it as "storehouse consciousness." Professor Jeffrey Hopkins translates it as "the basis of all." I'm not trying to be pedantic here. If you want to relate to it as the substratum of awareness or the basis of all or the storehouse consciousness, that is fine; there is no problem there.

All our conscious processes depend upon the substratum of awareness. Everything comes from it and dissolves somewhat back into it. We could almost say that it is a kind of unconscious—rather than a conscious state of mind—but if we were to say it is unconscious, that statement would be debatable in many ways. Even Western psychologists debate this. Sigmund Freud said there is some kind of unconscious state. Others say all our unconscious processes are really our own decision, that we don't like certain things so we make the choice not to be aware of those things, which is a conscious act in some sense. I think we could say the same thing here.

Yogacarin philosophers introduced the notion of the substratum of awareness for a reason. The Buddhist teachings are normally known as *atmavadin*, which means "no-self school" or "no-self tradition." Most Buddhist schools completely dispensed with the notion of a soul or self, but the Yogacarins (the people who expounded Yogacara philosophy) thought this really was not in keeping with our experience of our selves. We could say we are made up of nothing but our bodily constituents, thought process, and perceptions all jumbled together with no self or soul to unify the whole thing, but Yogacarin philosophers found this approach failed to really explain the problem of personal identity.

We think the person who had cornflakes in the morning is the same person who goes to bed that night. We do not think the person who had cornflakes in the morning is someone different to the person who is going to bed at night. Our thought processes take place in a temporal way. Thoughts come and go, perceptions come and go, but there is some kind of unifying process whereby we are aware we are the same person through and through. So the Yogacarins said there is a basic state of consciousness that actually continues.

There is also the problem—if you want to look at it that way—of what happens when we die. If we believe in rebirth, there must be some kind of basic principle that goes through and gets reborn. Yogacarins said we can't take rebirth unless there is some kind of basic principle—such as *alaya-vijnana* or "substratum of awareness"—responsible for our rebirth. We have to believe in some kind of substratum of awareness or consciousness to really explain the rebirth process; the fact of our memory, personal identity, and so on. The postulation of this substratum was not therefore done arbitrarily.

EGOCENTRIC MENTATION

Yogacarins also tried to provide a description of the evolution of consciousness. They felt that our whole conscious process is evolutionary in that we begin from some kind of primitive and unsophisticated level and develop more sophisticated states of mind. There is the basic substratum of awareness and then further growth takes place. This is known as *manovijnana*, which we could translate as "egocentric mentation." Egocentric we all know, while *mentation* comes from the Latin and means "act of the mind" so *egocentric mentation* means "egocentric acts of the mind."

Further growth takes place on this second level of consciousness. The alaya-vijnana begins to split into two regions: the reflecting side of the consciousness (*mano-vijnana*) and the region it reflects upon. These two sides of consciousness begin to develop on this level. Most of our egocentric activities revolve around this second level of consciousness and Yogacarins talk about three specific notions that are related to this particular mental state.

First, the belief that we have a soul or a self gets generated on this second level of consciousness because it mistakenly thinks the substratum of awareness is our soul or self. Second, arrogance is also related to this second level of consciousness, because all our pride—thoughts of how fantastic or terrific we are—get generated here. This includes thinking how terrible or bad we are, because we would not disparage ourselves unless we were egocentric, so that is also a form of arrogance. And third, the obsessive concern with oneself comes in here also because we can't look at anything without using ourselves as a reference point. This is really related to most of our activities because whatever we engage in, we always refer back to ourselves.

EMPIRICAL CONSCIOUSNESS

A third and final level of consciousness begins to develop when we give rise to the six sense organs. We have the five sensory organs of eyes, nose, ears, tongue, and touch, which everyone in Western traditions are familiar with, but the Buddhist context also acknowledges a sixth sensory organ: the intellectual or empirical mind. The six sense fields begin to develop from here as well. This is the last stage of the full development of consciousness and is called *pravrtti-vijnana*, which could be translated as "empirical consciousness."

When this whole process has taken place, consciousness is fully developed and all kinds of neuroses and emotional instabilities arise because of dualistic fixation. We believe there is an object out there and a subject in here, and begin to respond in ways that create all kinds of neurotic tendencies, which the Yogacarins call *vasanas* or "traces and dispositions."

Most of our interactions with the world really depend upon the interaction between the third level of consciousness (*pravrtti-vijnana*), which consists of the six sense organs and the six sense fields, and the substratum of awareness (*alaya-vijnana*), which is that relatively unconscious level. Whatever information the third stage of consciousness receives will be filtered through the level of our egocentric mentation (*manovijnana*) before it is recorded in the substratum of awareness. Egocentric mentation is where everything gets edited and placed into proper perspective and then that information is fed into the unconscious memory banks of the substratum of awareness.

Our senses might get stimulated by a particular "sensory object" (*alambana*) and that information is carried to the second level of consciousness, which performs some editing and then feeds that information into the substratum of awareness. This leaves traces and dispositions on the substratum of awareness, which then force us to act in particular ways. The whole thing begins to become a habitual process. We act in a particular way, which again leaves traces and dispositions in our substratum, and further reinforces our compulsion to act in a particular way. We continue that indefinitely and this is known as *samsara* or "going in cycles." This is the state of bondage in some sense because we are totally bewildered. In Christian terminology it might be called the "condemned state."

Even though the substratum of awareness is perceived as a kind of persisting principle it is not eternal. It is not like a soul that exists eternally, because the substratum of awareness also goes through changes; it also goes through temporal processes. It is said that when we attain enlightenment this substratum of awareness comes to an end. Once the content of the substratum of awareness is exhausted, we begin to develop a new kind of substratum of awareness. It continues that way instead of remaining the same old substratum of awareness that will persist indefinitely. The second level of consciousness does not operate when we are unconscious or asleep, we have to perform a deliberate act for there to be egocentric mentation and when we attain enlightenment this level of consciousness also begins to disappear. As long as there is interaction between the three levels of consciousness accompanied by some kind of fixation on subjectivity and objectivity, there will be a continuous process taking place. We do one thing, that leads to another, and that leads to another. An indefinite process takes place and this is what is known as samsara. This process can be stopped by employing a certain kind of method. We will discuss this method in the following chapters.

QUESTIONS

QUESTION: Was the atman one of the two notions the Yogacarins had?

RINPOCHE: In a Hindu context, *atman* normally means "self" or "soul," or something like that. Here atman is related to any kind of subjective experience. We don't have to infer about our own subjective experiences because we experience them directly. Anything that we have to use inference for is the objective side, which is dharma. The objective side is what we actually experience. We might have to use inference or we might not, it depends on whether it's taking place in our own mind. If we experience a table, then that is outside our experience in some sense. We directly experience a toothache or a headache, but it is experienced, so there is some kind of objective side. It could be physical or mental depending on the situation.

QUESTION: I missed the point of why of you referred to atman and dharma.

RINPOCHE: The whole process of the three levels of consciousness is related to atman and dharma, subject and object. The interaction between the three levels of consciousness is related to subject and object through and through, to the person and their world. At the same time the objective level includes a person's thought process as well. Thought and what is being thought about. Aggression and what a person is aggressive about. Aggression is the subjective side and what you are aggressive about is the objective side, so it is really the person and their view of the world. The world is on the objective side, the person is on the subjective side. That's atman and dharma. The whole thing is explained as a transformation of the conscious process.

QUESTION: Atman and dharma come from the alaya-vijnana so both are forms of consciousnes and basically the same?

RINPOCHE: That's right. We have to keep in mind that we are not talking about chairs and tables as they are. We're talking about how we experience chairs and tables. Sometimes people have interpreted Yogacarins to be saying that a chair is in your mind, a table is in your mind, everything is in your mind. Yogacara is really talking about how we experience these things. We're not talking about how they exist in themselves.

QUESTION: There is the Yogacarins statement of *cittamatra*, that there is "only mind."

RINPOCHE: Yogacarins put so much emphasis on the mind because they are concerned with practice. Some people think they were saying that everything is in your mind. Some of these people were influenced by certain Western philosophies. When Berkeley said, "Whatever you see or hear is in your own mind, it's all ideas," they thought, "This really makes sense." I think there is a problem here.

QUESTION: When you talk about "everything coming from the mind" are you talking about our reactions and perceptions of things?

RINPOCHE: That's right. We are not concerned about whether or not a chair exists. That's secondary. Why spend so much time arguing about whether or not a chair exists, instead of learning how we experience and relate to the chair, and what sort of experience we have got?

QUESTION: Egocentric mentation arises out of the substratum in a split. You were talking about reflecting on something?

RINPOCHE: What is reflected upon is the substratum of awareness. It splits into two regions. One section of the substratum of awareness is reflected by the other. There's the reflected side and the side that performs the act of reflection. Consciousness begins to develop into these two regions. We might experience pain. The pain, which is the objective side, is experienced by the subjective side. So it begins to develop into two kinds of regions, which is a split of some kind on the fundamental level.

QUESTION: Does a new substratum start after that? They say samsara is endless. Is that what it means?

RINPOCHE: It's not endless as much as indefinite. Endless means it's going to continue forever. Indefinite means it could stop any minute.

QUESTION: If buddhas exhaust their subconscious, what is the function of memory?

RINPOCHE: When there's a substratum of awareness, an unconscious state of mind, there is a dark corner we don't know about. We cannot be aware of this aspect at all. In many ways, it's totally ambiguous. An enlightened person becomes aware of this so the unconscious aspect begins to become exhausted of its contents. That doesn't make you an amnesiac who can't remember anything. Because you are aware, totally aware, there's no problem at all. In a way it's an evolutionary process. It starts from an indefinite state of mind: the substratum of awareness. That's not so much an enlightened state as a state of unawareness. A split takes place and you come into samsaric existence. Then you go through a whole process and the more you become aware of yourself, the more you are able to approach the goal, or whatever you want to call it. Any evolutionary process has a goal. A simple organism develops into a more complicated organism. A physicist might study atoms and finds it's more complicated than that. There is always an evolutionary process taking place on some level.

QUESTION: Is the "substratum of awareness" a term that is only applies to confused or unenlightened people?

RINPOCHE: In a way, because it is our own inner act. That's what I meant when I said it's a conscious decision in some sense to not be aware of ourselves. We ignore certain aspects of our own consciousness, and that's a conscious decision on some level. It's not unconscious in the ultimate sense. Resolution of that means becoming aware. That's what meditation is supposed to be: learning how to explore the dark corners of our consciousness. We should not run away from them or try to ignore them, but just explore our consciousness as much as we can.

QUESTION: You said something about emotional instability developing because of dualistic fixation.

RINPOCHE: Dualistic fixation is related to the second level of consciousness, because that's where all egocentric activities happen. There is a sharp distinction between you and other.

QUESTION: Are we born with the substratum?

RINPOCHE: It's due to the substratum of awareness that we are born. That is really what compels us to take rebirth. And it persists after death.

QUESTION: What exists before the substratum comes to be?

RINPOCHE: Buddhists would say that question is in some ways a self-defeating exercise. We could argue about whether the chicken or the egg came first. We can theorize about whether "I" came first or the "substratum of awareness" came first, but that doesn't really help us. That is why Buddhists say it is "beginningless." This doesn't really mean it is literally beginningless; it just means that it's indefinite. We could attain buddhahood if we choose to; we can work on ourselves and attain buddhahood, a fully enlightened state. It's not predetermined that we must continue to take rebirth forever. We start off with the substratum of awareness and go from there. A Buddhist would say that the substratum of awareness exists due to our own ignorance or lack of awareness.

QUESTION: What is it that is aware of the substratum?

RINPOCHE: It's the conscious side of it. We try to develop the third level of consciousness as much as we can. We begin to explore our consciousness, both the conscious and unconscious sections. We have to learn how to be completely aware of these things. It's a matter of developing the section or the region that we are aware of in normal circumstances. We could expand that as we go along.

QUESTION: I thought that some type of egocentric mentation would not be dissolved after death.

RINPOCHE: After death? No, when you are unconscious or when you are sleeping, egocentric mentation does not operate. That does not mean it has ceased to function completely, it just means it has ceased to function temporarily. It is dormant. In order for there to be egocentric mentation there has to be some kind of deliberate act involved.

QUESTION: Are the images that come up in dreams symbolic of our egocentric action?

RINPOCHE: In some ways, yes, but that is precisely the point: you can't choose to have a dream. You can't say, "I've had a hard day, I'm going to have a really good dream tonight." Whatever takes place when you are asleep is really related to the unconscious side of your consciousness, rather than your conscious side.

QUESTION: We are never going to perceive anything as it is, are we? We always going to operate from the preconceptions of the storehouse consciousness and think, "This is real."

RINPOCHE: That's right; that is our own confusion, in a sense.

QUESTION: How can you work through this process when you are at the end point of delusion? You've gone through the whole process wrongly.

RINPOCHE: Not necessarily. In meditation, for instance, what you do is see how your sense organs are stimulated by certain things. On the intellectual level, there might be a certain thought process or emotional state that disturbs you. You begin to learn how that actually disturbs you, how that actually stimulates your responses. Then you see how the whole thing gets filtered through your egocentric mentation. It's not hard. We just look at it and see how we add certain things. Projection is part of editing in many ways. We look at a certain situation and don't see it as it is, we see it as we want to see it. We project onto it certain things which are not there. That comes from the editing process that takes place within our mind. We begin to inquire further and further into the whole process.

QUESTION: You were describing the whole process as samsaric. Is the substratum the source of nirvana as well?

RINPOCHE: Yes; it gets transmuted. We begin to discover that the substratum of awareness is not our self. As we said, the second level of consciousness mistakenly holds the substratum of awareness to be the soul. It says, "This is me; this is my soul." Once we begin to dispense with that notion, we gradually discover that it's not our soul. In fact it contains a tremendous intelligence. It's a self-awakened state in some sense. We also start to discover that there aren't really three levels of consciousness. But I think if we discuss this now, we will only get confused.

QUESTION: I can't see the difference between the Buddhist notion of alaya-vijnana and the Hindu "soul" concept. The only distinction is that the alaya-vijnana changes all the time.

RINPOCHE: The difference is that the substratum of awareness cannot exist without its content. Our traces and dispositions are stored up. Once they get exhausted, another alaya-vijnana develops, rather than the same old thing that is persisting throughout. In some sense, the alaya-vijnana has a larger scale of persistency than the other levels of consciousness. But still, the alaya-vijnana itself is temporal. It is temporal, despite its persistence. Every minute, our cells are dying and getting replaced, but then there's you. You live on until you die, but your cells are dying and getting replaced every minute. It's a similar thing. We have thought processes, images and so on, that are related to all kinds of conscious processes, but then there's the substratum of awareness which persists for a time.

QUESTION: Are you saying the alaya-vijnana is not a thing, it's just a process?

RINPOCHE: It's a substratum where the whole thing is stored. But it can only exist if there are contents for it. It can't exist without the contents.

QUESTION: Where did the contents come from?

RINPOCHE: The contents come from the interaction between the alaya-vijnana and the empirical consciousness, and the interactions between the three levels of consciousness. You leave certain traces and dispositions that compel you to act in a particular emotive way, and that again leaves traces and dispositions so that you again act that way. The process continues in that way. It becomes a habitual process, which is known as *vasana* in Sanskrit or *bag chag* in Tibetan.

QUESTION: If you develop to the stage of a buddha, what would you be aware of?

RINPOCHE: A buddha is not obsessively concerned with his or her own self. That's the difference. If you get knocked out you think, "Someone knocked me out; this is me." That very act itself would be egocentric mentation. Believing that you are the same person would be to believe in the existence of the substratum of awareness. A buddha might not have those kinds of concerns.

QUESTION: How does the notion of alaya-vijnana relate to the notion of dharmakaya?

RINPOCHE: The purified state of alaya-vijnana would be dharmakaya.

QUESTION: If someone has a feeling that they are not very wholesome, isn't that a motivation to improve themselves?

RINPOCHE: That's right; that's why it's part of the arrogance of self. There are three aspects of egocentric mentation. The arrogance of self is the second one, which is either feeling good about yourself or feeling terrible about yourself and wanting to improve yourself.

QUESTION: So a sense of wanting to improve oneself is not particularly wholesome?

RINPOCHE: It is wholesome. What this means is that normally we begin to become neurotic. If you really detest yourself or become suicidal, that is neurotic; it's not healthy at all. But if you want to develop yourself in a healthy way, there's no problem there. It's not so much wanting to develop that is a problem, it is hating yourself, thinking the whole thing has come to an end and there is no point in continuing.

QUESTION: And that's not any different from pride?

RINPOCHE: It is pride. It is an expression of pride. That's how a Buddhist would see it. It's still concerned with you. Your pride is crushed. It's all concerned with your own well-being in a negative way. If it's done in a positive way, then that's no problem. Even wanting to attain buddhahood is part of a self-growth process. Wanting to improve yourself is okay as long as it doesn't become a neurotic preoccupation. But if you become preoccupied with the whole thing, it becomes a self-defeating process. That would be part of egocentric mentation.

Question: It's like having a boat on a river using the wind. After a while, you realize you could use this strong undercurrent which has a self-sustaining energy.

Rinpoche: In some sense, yes. Discovering what is already there, rather than trying to manufacture something, which is what we normally tend to do. If we try to improve ourselves in a neurotic way, we will be trying to manufacture something rather than to discover something. We are not making any discoveries; we are just producing unnecessary excess luggage.

Question: How can we know the contents of the substratum if that knowledge has been filtered by consciousness?

Rinpoche: The best way to find out is through doing meditation. At the same time, we have to pay attention to how we relate to things in an ordinary sense. We don't necessarily have to sit in meditative posture, but whenever we have time, we could see how we relate to things, how all these different levels of mind operate. By doing that we could see the whole operation.

Question: What about the reliability of what I come to understand from observation? That's being filtered through my consciousness.

Rinpoche: I think reliability depends on your own biases. The less biased you are about the whole thing, the more reliable it would be. Sometimes we feel we are really getting something out of it and then we become totally excited or neurotic and lose whatever we gained in some sense. If we are less biased and less emotionally involved with the whole situation, we will see it from a much better perspective.

Question: There seems to be a dilemma in recognizing the nature of the substratum because that is another interpretation.

RINPOCHE: No, I think whatever we experience really comes from that. Whatever we do leaves traces and dispositions there. For instance, if you just sit down and for no reason suddenly remember that when you were six you were reading Robinson Crusoe, that would be part of the traces and dispositions, part of the substratum of awareness, operating on that level. There was no external situation or stimulus to provoke that response. You just happen to suddenly discover or realize that you are thinking about it. You could remember something that took place three months ago. For no reason, you just happen to contemplate it. If we experience these things, we need to explore further.

QUESTION: I'd always thought that spontaneous insight was actually reprocessed or edited in order to make sense of it. You're talking about it a bit differently.

RINPOCHE: I think so. If we thought, "That's nothing, I just happened to stumble on it," then we wouldn't know anything. There might be some kind of interpretation involved, but still we are learning. We are learning why certain things are happening, which is important.

QUESTION: How do the three levels of consciousness relate to the superego, ego, and id?

RINPOCHE: I don't know very much about psychoanalysis, but I would imagine that those three would be related with egocentric mentation, the second level of consciousness. But there's no conflict between the three Buddhist aspects of egocentric mentation. In Freudian psychology, the id, ego, and superego are always fighting among themselves. The id is saying, "I want to do this" and the superego is saying, "Cool down, take it easy." All kinds of processes of that nature are said to be taking place.

QUESTION: Do you think that there's more internal conflict in the Western way of life than in the Eastern way of life?

RINPOCHE: I don't think that is necessarily so. I think this is universal. I think this takes place in any culture. There are always two sides to human beings: a primitive side which is instinctive and a developed side which is more rational. Whenever instinct tells you something, you can look at it and say, "Cool down." You can do that. It's as simple as that.

QUESTION: You seem to be saying, "Trust in your own experience," yet that experience is coming from a deluded state. How can you trust your judgment about whether you are progressing or how the mind works if you're suspicious about the whole mechanism to start with?

RINPOCHE: You have to be critical, and at the same time, you have to trust your own judgment. These two things go together. I don't think that they are contradictory. You make a judgment and then you critically judge it. You critically judge your own judgment. In some sense that has to be the process. Otherwise you would end up a skeptic. You would become suspicious of everything. Descartes doubted everything that was external to him. He doubted anything that wasn't in his consciousness. He couldn't believe in anything. Hume, the great Anglo-Saxon philosopher, doubted even himself. If you really doubt everything, you end up not being able to make any kind of judgment whatsoever. If you don't doubt anything, then you become a dogmatist. Buddhists say you have to have a middle way with whatever you do.

QUESTION: So if you have a reasonable doubt, you'd still work with it?

RINPOCHE: That's right. You can doubt everything. You could say, "How do I know that I'm seeing a table?" "How do I know I am experiencing aggression?" "There's nothing there. It's just a flash of something, it comes and goes. There's nothing there." You could go on and on indefinitely. There has to be some kind of middle approach.

QUESTION: Are you saying that the idea of doubt comes about because there's an object and a subject?

RINPOCHE: Yes. That's right.

QUESTION: I was thinking of the unconscious as an object, as something that my conscious observed. If I don't think of it like that, if it's just there, then that dilemma's gone.

RINPOCHE: That's precisely it. We can't become dogmatic and say that there is an object in our mental process or in the physical situation, there is something out there, and believe in it and become dogmatic about the whole thing. And we cannot doubt the whole thing and end up being a skeptic. We need to question but not end up a skeptic. Either way, we don't learn anything. If we become dogmatic we don't learn anything; if we become a skeptic we don't learn anything either. We end up being a skeptic because we doubt everything. If we doubt, that means we haven't any knowledge.

QUESTION: You could get very attached to the unconscious as you might to an object.

RINPOCHE: That's right; and that would produce more traces and dispositions so the process would continue indefinitely.

QUESTION: Does the alaya-vijnana exist within the mind or does it exist relative to the phenomenal world?

RINPOCHE: The substratum of awareness is linked with both: with yourself and with your experience of the world. Not so much the world as it is, but how you experience the world.

QUESTION: Is the alaya-vijnana related to the sense of self or ego? Without that sense of self, there's no alaya-vijnana?

RINPOCHE: Let's say that the substratum of awareness does not depend upon the other consciousnesses. The other conscious processes depend upon the substratum of awareness.

QUESTION: There seem to be blind spots related to the substratum of awareness. Those blind spots need to be investigated.

RINPOCHE: That's right; and there might be some kind of resistance on your part due to egocentric mentation. You might not want to explore certain things. You might choose not to.

QUESTION: How is that resistance made less resistant?

RINPOCHE: Through meditation, obviously, and through properly observing ourselves. That's what this whole thing is all about. Normally, we don't really want to observe anything about ourselves. If we have nothing to do, we want to go out, or we choose to do something or other rather than look at what is really taking place.

QUESTION: If you start to experience some blind spot when you're walking down the street, will that blind spot reoccur during your practice sessions or does it occur only when you're going through some activity?

RINPOCHE: It's taking place most of the time. You need to sit down whenever you can and just observe. It's as simple as that. You don't need to feel left out by the fact that you're walking down the street.

Three Constitutive Principles of Reality

I would like to introduce a few concepts that will enhance our understanding of the following chapters. This subject matter is not discussed in any great detail in the *Abhidharmasamuccaya*, but the text does make reference to it. Having a general idea of these concepts will make it easier for us to understand the ensuing discussions. We have introduced the notion of the evolution of consciousness in three levels of transformation of consciousness. The ideas in this chapter are also tied up with that in a way. There are three concepts that we need to become familiar with, and these are known as the three constitutive principles: *parinispanna-svabhava*, the "ideally absolute"; *paratantra-svabhava*, the "relative"; and *parikalpita-svabhava*, "the notional-conceptual."

We are in some sense concerned with metaphysics here. While we will not go into great detail about these three principles, we will have occasion to make reference to them as we go along so you should try to familiarize yourself with them.

The ideally absolute (*parinispanna-svabhava*) is that state of ourselves where there is no longer any distinction between subject and object, between experience and what is experienced: there is just an indeterminate state free from duality of subject and object. The relative (*paratantra-svabhava*) begins to operate when we become self-conscious and give rise to the perception of duality. When we go beyond the substratum of awareness and enter into the transformation of consciousness, the relative has begun to take place. The notional-conceptual (*parikalpita-svabhava*) is related to the belief in subject and object—subject and object are constructed on the relative. The relative does not really contain any subject and object, but subject and object are constructed upon it due to the notional-conceptual.

We could say the ideally absolute is the state of nirvana, and the relative and notional-conceptual are the samsaric mentality that we experience continuously. Nevertheless, the relative is the ideally absolute, but due to the habitual patterns of our notional-conceptual mind, the ideally absolute is mismanaged and we are unable to perceive it. The ideally absolute is seen in the form of subject and object: which is the relative principle. When subject and object are removed, the relative reveals itself to be the ideally absolute.

As we can see, of the three constitutive principles, the most important is the relative because it is responsible for the transformation of consciousness. All the levels of transformation we have so far discussed come under the auspices of the relative. The relative is therefore the basis of both samsara and nirvana. We either attain enlightenment or we go astray by becoming involved in the notional-conceptual.

These three principles are traditionally conveyed by the simile of a magician creating an elephant. A magician utters an incantation over a piece of wood and the spectators under the influence of that incantation perceive the wood to be an elephant. The perception of the elephant is the notional-conceptual. The way the elephant appears—which depends upon the incantation, the wood, and the magician, and so on—is the relative. When the influence of the incantation begins to wear off, the spectators begin to see the wood as it is, which is the ideally absolute. The ideally absolute is what is left behind when all the other things are exhausted.

In a similar way, the substratum of awareness—and the traces and dispositions that are stored up within it—make us perceive everything in terms of subject and object. That subject and object do not exist. They are simply constructed upon the relative and we do not realize that the relative itself is the ideally absolute. However, once the relative is purified of the dualistic notion of subject and object, it reveals itself to be the ideally absolute.

Everything we experience is put under the headings of "subject" and "object." The whole purpose of practice, if you like, is to remove that. The ideally absolute is revealed and discovered as neither subjective nor objective. In other words, the ideally absolute is not one particular individual's state of mind nor an objective thing to be discovered. It is revealed as a state of mind where there is no distinction between the object that has to be apprehended and the subject who apprehends it. This is the most metaphysical aspect of the whole thing and becoming familiar with these concepts will make it easier to understand the following chapters.

QUESTIONS

QUESTION: What are the Tibetan terms for these principles?

RINPOCHE: The notional-conceptual is called *kün tag pa*, the relative is called *zhen gyi ba* and the ideally absolute is called *yön su drub pa*.

QUESTION: How do those differ from *kün dzob* (relatively real) and *dön dam* (ultimately real)?

RINPOCHE: The first two (the notional-conceptual and the relative) are kün dzob, the third one (the ideally absolute) is dön dam. Madhyamaka philosophy talks about absolute and relative truth. The relative and the notional-conceptual would be relative truth. The ideally absolute would be absolute truth.

QUESTION: Does the use of different language imply different connotations in Madhyamaka and Yogacara?

RINPOCHE: In Yogacara philosophy, the notional-conceptual is not just emptiness as the Madhyamikas say. The ideally absolute is also something that can be discovered and realized. In some ways, it's an experiential state; but at the same time there is something to be discovered. Yogacarins say that what the ideally absolute is empty of is subject and object. The ideally absolute itself is not empty. In Madhyamaka philosophy, the absolute itself is empty. In Yogacara philosophy, the ideally absolute is empty of the notional-conceptual, which is constructed on the relative. Once that is removed, then the ideally absolute is discovered. So the ideally absolute is revealed as a consciousness as well as *tathata* or "things as they are." When the substratum of awareness is purified, it no longer remains the basis where all the traces and dispositions are stored. It gets purified of all that so it can apprehend or perceive things in their true nature, properly. At the same time what is perceived—the real nature of things—and the purified form of the substratum of awareness are not seen as two different things as they are in ordinary experience. What is perceived and that which is doing the perceiving are not differentiated.

QUESTION: Is the experience of the ideally absolute the same as nondual awareness?

RINPOCHE: It is nondual awareness. You don't construct anything and you don't see everything in terms of subject and object so you see things in a different light. You no longer project your own dispositions and tendencies onto things. You see things "as they are," which means you no longer see things as something out there to be experienced or perceived while you are in here.

QUESTION: Does this arise from the *Surangama Sutra*?

RINPOCHE: Yes and the *Lankavatara Sutra*. The *Surangama Sutra* and the *Lankavatara Sutra* were the inspiration for Asanga and Vasubandhu to build their system of philosophy.

QUESTION: I'm unclear as to the relationship of the relative to the notional-conceptual.

RINPOCHE: The relative itself is the ideally absolute, but the notional-conceptual (which consists of all the habitual patterns) constructs subject and object dualism onto the relative. So you see it as that rather than as the ideally absolute. The notional-conceptual projects what is not there onto the relative so you do not see the relative in its original state. You have changed it; you have turned it into something else. The relative and the ideally absolute are not two different states; they are presented as two different things only because of the way we see it. On the relative level of everyday experience, we see it as relative. If we were to get enlightened, we would see it as ideally absolute. That's the only difference. To put it philosophically, it's an epistemological difference, not an ontological difference.

QUESTION: So the order of these three is logical rather than an evolution of one into another?

RINPOCHE: That's right. That evolution of consciousness really consists of the superimposition of subject and object onto the relative.

QUESTION: You call these the three constitutive principles, but constitutive principles of what?

RINPOCHE: They are the constitutive principles of reality. They are three grades of reality in some sense; in a hierarchical order. But two of them are really just conventional. They are everyday experience, but they do not exist in an ultimate sense. The ideally absolute exists in the ultimate sense.

QUESTION: Where does belief in a self and belief in dharmas come into this?

RINPOCHE: The twofold ego comes from the notional-conceptual, which is constructed upon the relative.

QUESTION: When you get rid of your conflicting emotions and belief in the self and dharmas, does that eliminate the third level or does it show the relative to be the absolute?

RINPOCHE: It shows the relative to be the absolute. Once the subject and object distinction is removed the relative is revealed as the ideally absolute.

QUESTION: Why say "when things become exhausted"?

RINPOCHE: They become exhausted of traces and dispositions. We see things in a dualistic manner, because traces and dispositions coerce us into acting in a neurotic way. That produces further neuroses and further traces and dispositions, so we continue to see the whole thing that way. Once the content of the substratum of awareness is exhausted, the substratum begins to reveal itself as the ideally absolute, within which there is no distinction between what is perceived and the conscious state that is doing the perceiving.

QUESTION: We automatically leave traces, so the process becomes perpetual. How can we exhaust a perpetual process?

RINPOCHE: That's what we have to discuss: how to exhaust this process. Hopefully, we will be able to do that. Why should there be traces and dispositions? Why should there be a substratum of awareness to begin with? In a way, this chapter is a digression from the main theme of the book, but I thought it was important to have some understanding of the metaphysical aspects of Yogacara philosophy. We will not be too concerned with this aspect because we are dealing with a psychological text not a metaphysically oriented one. Yogacara philosophy is a system so it has different texts that deal with different subjects.

QUESTION: From the relative level, is absolute truth realized through logic and intellect, or through meditation?

RINPOCHE: Both, but mainly through meditation.

QUESTION: How does all this relate to the state of a child? Are you talking about evolution as something we had once and are striving to reach again or didn't we have it before?

RINPOCHE: There's a long range evolution that takes place from one end of the scale to the other: ever since we came into existence until we attain enlightenment. There is also a short range evolution that takes place from childhood until we die. A child would be going through that type of intellectual development. At first the child wouldn't necessarily be aware of subject and object and then consciousness becomes more and more determinate and sophisticated. Evolution takes place in that way. We also carry certain traces and dispositions from former lives. If we go along with Buddhism, we have to see it that way. There would be genetic influences, as far as our growth is concerned, but at the same time there are also mental dispositions that modify our behavior. Not everything is genetic.

QUESTION: Does that mean there is a substratum of unconscious content in a baby?

RINPOCHE: Sure. What happens is that the baby begins to manipulate the traces and dispositions so that consciousness becomes more and more defined and determinate. As far as the other evolution is concerned, Buddhists would say a child genius would mostly be due to the accumulation of former dispositions rather than from purely biological causes. There is evolution on that level, which is on a higher scale.

QUESTION: If a newborn infant is not self-conscious and makes no distinction between subject and object, does that mean the Buddhist path seeks to return to the lost innocence of infancy?

RINPOCHE: I don't think we are trying to regain our innocence. It's about discovering how this whole evolution has taken place and where we have mismanaged certain things, and being able to integrate our consciousness. It has become so fragmented. *Vikalpa* or "conceptual paraphernalia" means that. The consciousness is in a way totally centerless, jumping all over the place without any real point around which the other conscious experiences can revolve.

QUESTION: If you realize the ideally absolute, how do you then relate to the notional-conceptual?

RINPOCHE: If you realize the ideally absolute, the notional-conceptual ceases to function. The notional-conceptual exists due to traces and dispositions, which are stored in the substratum of awareness. Cessation of the notional-conceptual is the same as cessation of traces and dispositions. The substratum of awareness begins to become contentless.

QUESTION: Are you saying there is no necessity for notional and conceptual activity?

RINPOCHE: Yes. Still, there might be subject and object, the cessation of the perception of subject and object does not mean everything just becomes one, that subject and object become one thing. The way we experience it begins to change. We don't make sharp distinctions, because the more we do so the more we respond in an emotive way. That leaves all kinds of impressions, which force us to act in an even more emotional way, and so it goes. But if we become less deterministic in our way of looking at the whole thing within a dualistic framework, we have more chance of seeing things as they are, rather than as we want to see them. In order to be able to see things as they are, we have to try to look at things in a less dualistic way, which at the same time cuts through our habitual patterns.

QUESTION: What's the difference between seeing things as they are and seeing things from an emotive point of view?

RINPOCHE: Normally, we see things in different ways because of our backgrounds. We don't see a thing in its entirety. For instance, if a person falls out of a window, a physicist might say it's the law of gravitation and a psychologist might say the person had a frustrated life so they jumped. People really see things in different ways. That is okay, but the more we are able to see things in a less subjective way, the more we will see things as they are, rather than interpreting them by using ourselves as a reference point.

QUESTION: If you are in a certain situation, but then start remembering things about another situation, are those memories just left over traces from that situation or is it possible those traces are seeing the situation as it is?

RINPOCHE: As long as there are traces and dispositions we will not see things in a real way. There might be degrees of validity to our perception, but as long as there are traces and dispositions, we will see things as a result of those influences rather than from a proper perspective.

QUESTION: Sometimes I perceive something less dualistically than others, when there seems to be some conflict between that and my being in the world.

RINPOCHE: Each individual really sees things in his or her own way. That is an ordinary experience. It is nothing special. But at the same time, there are possibilities of seeing things from a proper perspective. Sometimes, as you've said, we are able to see things in a less dualistic way, especially if we view art or appreciate the beauty of nature. That is a less dualistic way of looking at the whole thing. Sometimes there is the possibility of seeing whatever we are seeing in its entirety, rather than in the fragmented way that normally happens.

QUESTION: Does that mean that everyone who is enlightened sees a thing in the same way?

RINPOCHE: In a way, that is true, yes. A proper perspective means we don't have to see a thing as if it is "for us" or "against us," which tends to be our normal activity. Should I hug it and take it away or should I leave it and ignore it? Or we might build all kinds of resentment because of our past association with a particular object, whatever it is. Enlightened beings wouldn't necessarily see things in that kind of context—as either for or against them—but would just see things as they are.

QUESTION: If you look at what is happening as a third party that is not involved and can see the cause and the result of it, would that perception be less dualistic?

RINPOCHE: In a way, that's true. It shows us how the influence of our past association with certain situations modifies our behavior in a particular context. A third person would see the situation much more clearly than the people involved in it, because the situation is charged with all kinds of emotional overtones for those involved. If a third person is not emotionally entangled with the situation, he or she would be able to see things in a proper perspective.

QUESTION: If one doesn't react mentally, then karma isn't made?

RINPOCHE: That's right. I think that's what we try to learn in meditation. We are trying to become nonhabitual. When you meditate you might think your mind has to be calm. You have some presuppositions or assumptions about what meditation is supposed to be. If you feel aggressive in meditation, your instinct might be to respond aggressively toward your own aggression. You might think, "This is really bad, this shouldn't be happening." But in meditation we learn how not to respond in that kind of way. It could be that your meditation is progressing very well and you think you should not lose that state. You might grasp at that. You need to refrain from that kind of response as well. What you try to do is look at your own emotional state directly without reacting to it as you would in normal circumstances. You first practice that with your own emotional states before you do it with others.

QUESTION: So initially, there's got to be some removal of yourself from your immediate emotional reaction to be able to see situations properly?

RINPOCHE: Yes, you begin to observe your own emotional states.

QUESTION: Then later, when that is strengthened, you can utilize the full energy of the emotions without stepping back from them?

RINPOCHE: Yes, that comes later on when you really understand what emotions are about. Normally we are not able to learn about emotions. We instinctively react to our emotions in an emotional way and are unable to explore the nature of the emotions properly. We are unable to do that because we are already biased when we look at the whole thing. The more we are able to look at the emotions from an unbiased point of view, the more we can learn about the nature of the emotions, whereby we might discover that emotions are really not something terrible or bad.

Yogacara Proofs for the Evolution of Consciousness

The Yogacarins believe there are three levels of consciousness: an indeterminate conscious state, an egocentric state, and the consciousness of the six sense faculties (which also contain the experience of the objective side of those faculties). All these things are explained in terms of our own experience. Yogacarins are not much interested in whether the objects of our sense perceptions exist in an ultimate sense or not. They are much more interested in how we experience things. We are going to find out what sort of proofs they offer for these three levels of consciousness. This is important because we first need some kind of philosophical or psychological background for what the Yogacarins are trying to explain. Only then will we be able to translate that into our own spiritual growth and into the context of our meditative experiences. We have to know how Yogacarins tried to explain the mind, how it operates, and how it perceives the phenomenal world.

PROOFS FOR THE EXISTENCE OF ALAYA-VIJNANA

At the beginning, there is the *alaya-vijnana*, which I have translated along with Professor Guenther, as the "substratum of awareness." The alaya-vijnana is a totally indeterminate state of consciousness, which means that at this stage, our consciousness is neither virtuous nor nonvirtuous, neither psychologically wholesome nor psychologically unwholesome. It remains completely neutral and indeterminate in its characteristics but has the ability to retain traces and dispositions. Whatever we experience leaves some kind of impression on the substratum of awareness, which in turn coerces us to act in a particular manner, and that again makes it possible for us to leave further impression on the substratum. When those traces and dispositions get actualized, we will again act in a particular way so that the whole cycle begins to evolve in that manner.

The interpreters of Yogacara philosophies have disagreed somewhat on this point. Some have said that the traces and dispositions are completely indeterminate while others have said they are determinate. The tradition that we are following here suggests the traces and dispositions should be indeterminate. They should be indeterminate because whatever we do leaves impressions on the substratum of awareness, but on a dormant or potential level. When the traces and dispositions become actualized—when the potentials become actualized—whatever is implicit becomes explicit. There is a difference, because if the traces and dispositions were determinate there would not be any difference between them and our experience of them when they become actualized.

If we put this in karmic terms, we create good karma or bad karma and it leaves impressions on the substratum of awareness. If those impressions were determinate, the impressions themselves would be the same as our experience of karmic results. There would be no difference between the cause and the effect. What is suggested here is that in terms of our experience of the whole situation we would not be able to explain the difference between cause and effect unless we regard the cause and the potential state of the traces and dispositions as indeterminate and our experience of that as determinate. *Indeterminate* means that the traces and dispositions left on the substratum of awareness are not necessarily virtuous or nonvirtuous; they are completely undefined. They are not explicit but implicit. They become virtuous or nonvirtuous when we begin to experience them or when the whole thing gets actualized.

One proof offered for the existence of the substratum of awareness is that it has relative permanence, whereas all other conscious experiences are completely temporal. We may experience pain and we may experience pleasure, but one conscious experience gets continually replaced by another. Whatever we experience gets intercepted by some other experience. As we cannot explain our personal identity by that kind of conscious process, the Yogacarins say there must be a substratum of awareness that is the basis or possibility for all our other experiences to take place. Pain and pleasure and so on actually function due to the fact that we have a substratum of awareness. Our experiences of pain and pleasure also leave traces and dispositions on the substratum of awareness, which in turn creates more pain and pleasure. And so it goes. That is the Yogacarin way of explaining cyclic existence.

The substratum of awareness is not completely permanent, like a piece of stone or the sky. It is temporal, but it has relative permanence. A traditional analogy is that a stone has greater durability than a sesame seed, but the stone does not have any scent. The sesame seed, which has less durability than the stone, is perfumed. In a similar way, the substratum of awareness is not eternal, but because it has relative permanence, it is perfumed. It changes continuously as a previous state of the substratum can influence the next state. Nonetheless it has more durability than the rest of consciousness.

We now come to the stage where we can discuss the traces and dispositions. "Traces and dispositions" refer to the impressions that are left behind on the substratum of awareness. The Tibetan term for that is *bag chag*, where *bag* means "covered" or "camouflaged" and *chag* means "existing." So, *bag chag* means "existing in a camouflaged way." Our traces and dispositions are not experienced consciously; they are only experienced on an unconscious level, and so they are known as something that exists in a camouflaged way. The Sanskrit term vasana has the same kind of implication. It also means something like "perfuming," something that leaves behind traces and dispositions.

It is said that all kinds of traces and dispositions exist on the level of the substratum of awareness. We go through hundreds of experiences each day and they leave behind all kinds of impressions. However only certain impressions or traces and dispositions get actualized because it depends upon what stimulates a particular response. It might sound a bit modern but this is so. Traces and dispositions cannot get actualized randomly and without any kind of order. There is some order because certain situations provoke certain traces and dispositions and others provoke other traces and dispositions. There is no chaos. It is not as if any of the traces and dispositions could be actualized at any time and place so that the whole thing goes berserk. There is some order in terms of what gets actualized first. Then other potentialities can follow suit. There is some homogeneity in the interaction between the stimulant and the stimulus; they are not contradictory. An aggressive situation would provoke an aggressive response. If someone screams at you, then you will scream back at them ninety-nine per cent of the time. It is quite straightforward. That homogeneity is known as *gum tum* in Tibetan.

As mentioned, the traces and dispositions are completely indeterminate. We could take the example of sugar. Sugar itself is indeterminate in some sense; it is in a potential state. It could be put into a cup of tea or coffee or into a piece of cheesecake and it gets absorbed wherever it is applied. The application of the sugar determines the characteristic it will assume. If it is applied to cheesecake, it gets absorbed into the cheesecake. If applied to coffee, it gets absorbed into the coffee. In a similar way traces and dispositions are indeterminate, but what is indeterminate can become determinate, depending upon the external circumstances, just as the sugar gets influenced by a foreign element. The "indeterminate state" is called *lung ma ten*.

Another proof offered for the existence of the substratum of awareness is that unless there was such a substratum we would not be able to take rebirth. It is only because of the substratum of awareness that we are able to take rebirth. Buddhists have completely rejected the notion of atman or "soul" as expounded in the Hindu and most Occidental traditions, so unless there is a substratum of awareness there is no reason why there should be rebirth. As most of our conscious experiences are temporary, there is also no reason why there should be a personal identity. Why should a person take rebirth and experience the same things they have experienced in the past? It is the substratum of awareness that endures the experience of different lifetimes and is able to retain the traces and dispositions of previous lives. Sometimes we are able to recall certain incidents that took place in a previous life. Those memories can take place only because there is some kind of personal identity. It is not the soul, but the substratum of awareness, which is able to retain those memories.

There is a basic difference between the theistic notion of soul and Yogacarin notion of the substratum of awareness. According to the theistic tradition, the soul is eternal; it exists during our condemned state as well as when we are "redeemed" and begin to dwell in the heavenly realm. However according to Yogacara philosophy the substratum of awareness has only relative permanence. We must remember that it is not eternal. It does not persist indefinitely.

The third proof offered for the existence of the substratum of awareness is that when a person is in a coma or a state of amnesia something must rule the integrity of that personality. That must be the substratum of awareness because the rest of our conscious experience is not explicit. There must be some kind of unconscious level of personal identity that actually persists during those times. So the substratum must exist on that level.

PROOFS FOR THE EXISTENCE OF MANO-VIJNANA

The second development of consciousness is called egocentric mentation or mano-vijnana. This is the center of our conscious experience and our egocentric notions. Most of our philosophical and theological notions of the soul come from this particular experience. We feel that there is some kind of personality, some kind of soul, and this strong emotion comes from egocentric mentation. It is said that egocentric mentation is the level of consciousness that we have to deal with in our practice. If there was no egocentric mentation, there would be no neuroses and emotional instabilities. Practice therefore comes down to uprooting or making a proper assessment of egocentric mentation.

The first proof offered for the existence of egocentric mentation is that if it did not exist we would be completely altruistic. We would be able to constantly work for the benefit of others and not feel anything selfish. We feel selfish and egocentric most of the time because we have this particular aspect of consciousness.

The second proof is that when we enter into meditative absorption, where the sense faculties begin to cease and other types of conscious experience diminish somewhat, there is still strong egocentric activity. We might feel that our meditation has progressed so well we wonder how we actually achieved that state. This type of experience exists due to the egocentric mentation. We might think our conscious experiences have ceased but egocentric mentation is still operating and persisting throughout our meditative absorption. That does not have to be the case in all meditative states but it does happen.

The third proof is that unless egocentric mentation existed any wholesome acts we tried to perform would be totally immaculate and involve no emotional embellishments or overtones. To put that in Buddhist terms, if we try to create good karma by participating in prayers or meditation, it would automatically be immaculate. But that is not the case.

Sometimes we try to create good karma but it is not free from emotional overtones. Due to that fact, egocentric mentation is involved in the experience of spiritual practice.

In brief, it seems whenever we are concerned with ourselves, whenever it comes to subjective experiences, we will inevitably experience some form of egocentricity, which influences all the inputs we receive from the objective side. The whole thing gets processed that way so that we always make some kind of wrong assessment of the situation in the end. Firstly egocentric mentation mistakenly believes the substratum of awareness is our soul or ego. Secondly egocentric mentation mistakenly becomes obsessively concerned with our own ego. Thirdly egocentric mentation begins to develop a tremendous sense of arrogance, which includes being self-effacing and putting ourselves down. That is the second level of the development of consciousness.

THE SIX SENSE CONSCIOUSNESSES

The third development of consciousness, the empirical consciousness or *pravrtti-vijnana*, is actually quite straightforward and something we experience constantly. While the evolution we have presented so far is completely removed or remote from our daily experience, this third level of consciousness involves the way we perceive the world through our sense consciousnesses. According to Buddhist psychology, there are five consciousnesses that are related to the five senses, and there is a sixth consciousness called "empirical mind," which is the mind we normally experience. The five senses receive input from the five sense fields and the sixth consciousness is how we are able to perceive mental images.

The relationship between the three levels of consciousness is this: whatever input we have from our experience of the objective side is perceived by the six sense consciousnesses, and then the egocentric mentation performs some kind of editing process, which leaves traces and dispositions on the substratum of awareness. The whole process takes place in that order. When the traces and dispositions are actualized, they get processed through egocentric mentation and then enacted through the six sense consciousnesses. It goes both ways. First the input and then the output take place. As we can see egocentric mentation seems to be the central point in ordinary types of experience.

As we will discover, when we develop spiritually, egocentric mentation is completely dispensed with, the substratum of awareness is transformed, and the six sense consciousnesses remain as they are. They do not get transformed because they don't contain any emotional overtones. Egocentric mentation is responsible for wrong judgments and wrong assessments we tend to perform within ordinary experience. Once that is dispensed with, whatever we experience or perceive is going to be much more straightforward and clear.

This whole thing is going to become quite clear as we go along. It is important to have some intellectual understanding of the whole situation and what is taking place. Only then can we discuss how spiritual discipline begins to develop and how all the nice things on the spiritual path can come about.

QUESTIONS

QUESTION: What do you mean exactly by "determinate" and "indeterminate"?

RINPOCHE: *Determinate* means "karmically wholesome or unwholesome" and *indeterminate* means "neither wholesome nor unwholesome." If you are hungry and have a pizza, that would leave only indeterminate traces and dispositions.

QUESTION: Is the ability to remember things part of the substratum?

RINPOCHE: Yes, any memory that we have is related to the substratum of awareness.

QUESTION: If awareness is applied at the point when an emotional reaction is arising, wouldn't that bring clarity and not create new vasanas?

RINPOCHE: Yes, that's right. We will be discussing how we can stop that in subsequent chapters. First there are the six sense consciousnesses, then egocentric mentation, and then the substratum of awareness. In meditation we are trying to find out how that whole process takes place, which is not very difficult at all, in many ways.

QUESTION: Whatever we learn in meditation, we ultimately have to apply in our daily life. Would that be where one applies the awareness one might have developed in meditation?

RINPOCHE: I think so, yes. First we have to talk about it as we are doing tonight. In fact, we have to find out whether there are such things as the three levels of consciousness. We don't know. A lot of you might doubt the whole situation and there is no problem there. We have to explore and see whether there is such a thing as a substratum of awareness, if there is such a thing as egocentric mentation. We won't doubt the six sense consciousnesses because they are too immediate. But we have to see all three levels of consciousness and the only way we can do that is through meditation. If we can to see the whole thing in a much clearer way, we could apply that to daily life.

QUESTION: Where does the desire to become enlightened come from? Is it from the traces and disposition?

RINPOCHE: Yes, the desire to attain enlightenment also comes from certain traces and dispositions left behind from previous experiences. Not everyone feels that way, so there is a reason why we feel that way in a particular situation. According to Buddhist tradition it could be due to our previous lives.

QUESTION: You were saying the substratum is only relatively permanent. Does that mean at some point the substratum ceases to exist? Is that what we call enlightenment?

RINPOCHE: In some sense, it ceases to exist, but in some ways the substratum gets transformed into something positive. The substratum is indeterminate. There is no distinction between subject and object. That indeterminate state could be very vague and very confused, or it could be very sharp, completely perspicuous, and very straightforward. In our ordinary experience the substratum would be very vague and foggy. At the enlightened stage it is very sharp. There is no distinction between subject and object, but still there is tremendous clarity, so it gets transformed.

QUESTION: You lost me with the example of the sesame seed and the stone.

RINPOCHE: A stone has more durability than a sesame seed. The stone lasts relatively forever, whereas the sesame seed has only a temporary existence. In a similar way, the substratum of awareness has only relative permanence so it is not like the stone or the sky. Those are traditional analogies. If the substratum of awareness were eternal it wouldn't be able to contain any traces and dispositions. The reason it contains traces and dispositions is because it is going through certain transformations. You experience certain things that leave traces and dispositions and they get actualized due to certain circumstances. That actualization leaves further traces and dispositions and then they get actualized; it continues that way. The substratum of awareness could not be eternal as it is not something solid that exists forever. If it were eternal, you would not be able to become enlightened due to the fact that the substratum of awareness could not be transformed into something else. If it is eternal and solid, you cannot change it.

QUESTION: I can't understand the idea of relative permanence.

RINPOCHE: The sesame seed is something relatively impermanent. It is fresh and gives off a certain scent. A stone is quite permanent compared to the sesame seed and it is not something fresh. You can come across a stone that has existed for millions of years. This is quite a straightforward and dull analogy in some sense. Only something that is fresh and going through transformations would be able to retain traces. It therefore has to be a fresh process that is taking place constantly. At the same time, it is not completely impermanent, it has relative permanence. Our ordinary conscious experiences are totally impermanent. We experience pain and pleasure, ups and downs. We go through all that sort of thing every minute in most cases.

The substratum of awareness would not necessarily go through that scale of impermanence but still it is impermanent and not eternal. And because it is not eternal it is able to be transformed into wisdom. When you become enlightened, the substratum of awareness gets transformed into something that does not retain traces and dispositions anymore. Actually, it is not so much that the substratum of awareness doesn't retain traces and dispositions; the person does not leave any traces and dispositions. That person is able to perceive the substratum as it is. In some sense, egocentric mentation is acting as a veil that prevents us from coming to grips with the substratum of awareness. We are unable to come to grips with the unconscious state. The only way we will be able to do that is by working through egocentric mentation, which is the center of all our emotional and neurotic tendencies. That is what coerces us into constantly acting in the same way and developing all kinds of inveterate tendencies.

QUESTION: Would dream yoga be a way of exploring the substratum of awareness?

RINPOCHE: Very much so. The dream yoga of Tibetan Buddhism is really designed to see how egocentric mentation operates in terms of the editing processes. It is supposed to make you become aware in the dream state. You see how you get excited due to certain dream images, but there is really nothing to get excited about. That type of practice is supposed to make you see how you do that and the reason why you do that. According to Buddhism, dream images are nothing but the traces and dispositions of our waking, conscious, experiences. In the dream state, those things get actualized, in some sense. We have to learn how those things take place and how they are getting edited through our egocentric mentation.

QUESTION: The first moment that you perceive a flower, do you just experience it, and then in the next moment start to pile on all the concepts, "I like this, I don't like that." Is that first moment filtered through egocentric mentation?

RINPOCHE: Not necessarily, it could be due to the six sense consciousnesses. The six sense consciousnesses are indeterminate as well, actually. The substratum of awareness is also indeterminate. Egocentric mentation colors the whole vision. Egocentric mentation is the unwelcome guest who has chosen to inhibit us. Practice is really about trying to work through the unnecessary situation of having egocentric mentation; it is totally unnecessary. It seems to be that egocentric mentation is the center whereby we feel there is something out there and there is me in here. It's the origination of all dualistic experiences. That dualistic experience does not take place on the sensory or substratum level. It takes place on the level of egocentric mentation.

We make distinctions and put everything into pigeonholes, which makes it very difficult for us to see things in their entirety; we only see things in parts. All kinds of constructions take place that are not really there. They are not properties of the object we are experiencing; they are the contribution of our own mind. This contribution is not made by our senses; it is made by egocentric mentation. Sometimes we come into contact with certain situations and we see the whole situation properly and think everything is really clear and in perspective. However, the more we try to look at it and make a proper assessment of it, the more complicated it becomes. We may come up with some kind of clever answer that creates further complications. It goes that way.

QUESTION: You see a flower, which is the first contact, then you think it is beautiful or fragrant, which is egocentric consciousness. My experience is that if no reaction arises by just seeing something, it is like being a zombie or a robot, which does not have the faculty of thinking. That would not be a clear mind either?

RINPOCHE: That is a very good question. We will discuss this in a later chapter when we talk about the five wisdoms. For example, we talk about "mirrorlike wisdom," which means your mind is like a mirror. Everything is reflected in it but the mind does not impose any kind of judgment on that reflection because any judgment that you could make is not related to any property of the object. Any judgment that you make would be the mind's own contribution to the object. It has nothing to do with the object you perceive. At the same time, that does not lead to any kind of vagueness. There is also what is known as "discriminating wisdom." Discriminating wisdom has nothing to do with seeing one object as better than another, you are able to make a proper assessment of every single object. You see the object from its own perspective without getting mixed up. It does not mean you see everything as the same and therefore everything is cool. There is distinction but that distinction is not imposed on the object by our own "conceptual paraphernalia" or *vikalpa*. It has nothing to do with conceptual paraphernalia. You simply begin to see things from their own perspective. Vikalpa is associated with egocentric mentation.

QUESTION: Does every experience arises from the vasanas?

RINPOCHE: Somewhat, but there are degrees of *vasanas* or "traces and dispositions." Sometimes our perception is less influenced by our traces and dispositions than others. The more emotional we are, the more our perception is influenced by vasanas. That is what it all boils down to. If we are emotionally charged in a given situation, we would see things in a distorted manner. The less our perception is charged with emotion, the less we would see things in that self-distorted way. I don't think every perception is distorted by traces and dispositions. Some perceptions could be quite clear. That also takes place occasionally but it is not a daily experience. That is what we are discussing. Also the substratum of awareness is the seat of enlightenment. It is not just the seat of samsara and of getting confused; it is the key to enlightenment at the same time. This is something very personal. It is something we experience constantly. It is not something that is remote and inaccessible.

QUESTION: What do you mean by "mentation"?

RINPOCHE: *Mentation* just means "mental act." Egocentric mentation means "egocentric mental act." It simply means being egocentric, egocentric thinking. Anything to do with "I" or "me" is egocentric mentation. Such as when you go to a cafe and get a diluted cup of coffee and say, "I didn't get my money's worth."

QUESTION: How does anything exist without having any sort of distinguishing characteristic? People have characteristics which distinguish them from each other. Is that related to egocentric mentation?

RINPOCHE: Not necessarily. When we talk about working through our habitual patterns, it doesn't mean we all become the same, that we all operate the same way. Enlightened beings would not necessarily operate in the same way as each other. There is no uniform activity. Shakyamuni Buddha was a monk, but the coming Buddha is not supposed to be a monk. Instead of sitting cross-legged under a Bodhi tree, he is depicted as sitting on a chair, which is very modernized, very proper. We cannot think that all these beings act in the same way. Enlightenment does not mean that everybody begins to behave the same. All it means is that we do not make the same mistakes and errors again and again, which is what we normally tend to do. Normally we feel, "Wherever I go things are the same. It doesn't make any difference. Wherever I go there are problems." If we look inside, we might begin to learn more things. Instead of thinking, "There are problems all around me," you might ask, "Why is it that some people don't experience problems in certain circumstances but do experience them in others?" You might experience problems in some circumstance while other people do not, but they do experience problems in other circumstances. There is some kind of habitual, inbuilt, tendency to react in a particular way due to our own inveterate tendencies.

QUESTION: "Inveterate tendencies" refers to when somebody screams at you and you scream back?

RINPOCHE: That and our own idiosyncratic way of responding to things, our own individual style of responding to things. We have accumulated those things as well, which has something to do with the traces and dispositions we were talking about.

QUESTION: So if you're involved in a situation that is very emotionally charged, it's your reaction at that time that counts. If someone screams at me, is it my reaction that matters more than anything else?

RINPOCHE: You have to make a proper assessment of why that particular person is behaving like that. At the same time, you have to understand how you are responding to it and how you have responded to that type of situation in the past. A lot of the time we don't want to look into the situation in terms of our own motivations and behavior. We might think, "All people are the same; they are all creating problems for me." We have to see why we are responding the way we do. It is a common problem and it depends on the contents of the substratum of awareness. Traces and dispositions are built up there and we respond the way that we do as a result of them. What we will discuss in the following chapters is really some kind of unlearning process.

QUESTION: "The substratum of awareness is indeterminate and traces and dispositions require stimulants to arise." Doesn't that statement imply dependent origination, which would mean that in the ultimate sense it is unreal?

RINPOCHE: Yes, that's right. If we put it in the metaphysical context that we talked about in the previous chapter, it comes under the relative and the notional-conceptual. They are not really real, in an ultimate sense. When we are talking about Yogacarin metaphysics, "the relative" really means things depend upon each other. Subject depends upon object. What is the subject if there is no object to be perceived? What is the perceiver? It doesn't make any sense. An object without a perceiver is useless. If there is a world without any sentient beings to perceive it, that world has no function whatsoever. Objects depend upon each other, so that is the relative. But the very fact that they depend upon each other means they are not real, because what is real is completely independent. What is independent is the ideally absolute, which is the substratum of awareness, because it does not depend upon subject and object. That would be to put it in a metaphysical context.

QUESTION: Is this breakdown applicable to all schools of Buddhism?

RINPOCHE: It is particular to Yogacara philosophy, both in a metaphysical sense and a psychological sense. The eight levels of consciousness, six levels of reality, and three constitutive principles are very much a Yogacara way of presenting the whole thing. Most Buddhists talk about two levels of truth: absolute and relative truth. It doesn't matter what school of Buddhism it is. They only refer to six levels of consciousness also—never to eight levels of consciousness—and these six consciousnesses refer to the five sense consciousnesses and the empirical consciousness (the mind we are normally in contact with). When we see something, the empirical level of our consciousness thinks, "That is an object of some sort." Whatever we perceive, it is the consciousness that makes a proper assessment of it. There's just these six consciousnesses in most Buddhist presentations. The Yogacara has eight levels of consciousness: these six, and then egocentric mentation, and the substratum of awareness. The interesting thing is that the Yogacarin philosophers were the people that really meditated and practiced in India. Not that other Buddhists did not meditate and practice, but at some stage people were getting intellectually rigorous and were not practicing very much. Yogacara philosophy developed out of that kind of practice-orientated background. Yogacara literally means "practitioners of yoga." It doesn't have anything to do with yoga as we normally understand it—bending backward or forward and so forth—but with doing meditation and with applying some kind of introspective method to observe our own conscious experiences.

QUESTION: If this is the teaching of Buddha, how can it be Yogacara philosophy alone?

RINPOCHE: Buddhist tradition, like everything else, has gone through stages and some sophistication has developed gradually due to that. The basic principles are the same whatever Buddhist school we refer to. Early Buddhism emphasized the object as well as the subject in equal measure. If we put it in a more technical way, we could say there was the same emphasis on matter and mind. Then Madhyamaka philosophy came along and said that mind and matter are equally unreal. They are both "empty," both *shunyata*. Yogacara philosophy put more emphasis on experience and mind than it did on the objective side. It didn't deny the existence of the object; it just said that it is useless to speculate about the existence of the world if we don't know what it is. We have to find out how we *experience* the world. The whole thing is very much related to personal experience. That led to the development of Buddhist tantra, which is the culmination of the Buddhist tradition. Zen came out of Yogacara philosophy also and is also somewhat related to the tantric tradition. The tantric tradition was the final development of Buddhism and I think a certain understanding of Yogacara would enhance your understanding of tantra. The tantric tradition tries to combine Madhyamaka and Yogacara philosophy with some bias toward Yogacara.

Whatever you might think of the proofs offered by the Yogacarins in defense of the existence of three levels of consciousness, you should appreciate the fact that they at least tried to offer them without asserting the whole thing in a dogmatic way.

Five Skandhas

We are now going to discuss the classic Buddhist notion of the five skandhas. Some of you might think you have the five skandhas coming out of your ears because you have heard about them so much, but the way the five skandhas are interpreted by the Yogacarins is slightly different from the standard Buddhist interpretation. We could also look at them in the context of the general Yogacara framework. The *five skandhas* could be translated as "five psychophysical constituents." If you want to reduce that, they come under the heading of "name and form." This is a standard Buddhist contention. *Name* does not mean the name we possess but stands for "consciousness" and *form* stands for "the body." So there is some kind of mind-body problem here.

The mind-body problem has been dealt with in the Western tradition quite thoroughly. Most of the time—ever since Plato—people regard the body as something bad and worthless because it is mutable and the soul as something worthwhile and to be cherished because it is immortal and resides in the body. In the West a lot of theories are offered about the relationship between mind and body. There is what is known as "the theory of psychophysical parallelism", which means the body is one thing and the mind another and they do not interact at all. They work like two clocks that just happen to exhibit the same time, without there being any visible relationship between the two. There is also "the theory of interactionism," which means that mind and body interact. That is how we normally see the situation I think, which is a common sense approach to the whole thing. Buddhists would go along with the idea that mind and body interact. An explanation is offered as to how they interact, but it is assumed that they do interact, and we normally take it to be so.

FORM

The first skandha is *rupa* or *zug*, "form." Whatever physical stature you possess is regarded as body. The body is different from consciousness. Body is not consciousness; a sense organ is not consciousness. We have to make a distinction between sense consciousness and sense organs. A sense organ is one thing and a sense consciousness is another. There are three things involved: you have a sense field, a sense organ, and a sense consciousness. All three things have to converge for you to have any kind of sense perception. When one of your sense organs is damaged, the sense consciousness and the sense field are still present, but you are unable to make a proper assessment of the situation due to your defective organ. The skandha of the body encompasses everything that is physical, including the brain, which is why we can't accept certain materialist interpretations of mind. We can't explain away mind by studying our brain processes or nerve endings, which is why Buddhists assume some version of the theory of interactionism. The mind and body interact with and depend upon each other, but at the same time, they are quite separate. If we tried to explain everything on the basis of physical things we would formulate a kind of psychophysical identity theory where the body and the mind are to be regarded as one thing.

Form refers to the body, but within the Yogacara system it includes almost everything, not just the physical sensory presentations but also ideal presentations. If you experience a drug-induced hallucination or see a mirage in the desert, it might be regarded as either something external or something mental, but as far as Yogacara is concerned it is "form" because it is experienced by the mind. Whether a particular sensory presentation is mind-dependent or independent of mind is totally secondary; whatever mind experiences is regarded as form. It doesn't matter whether sensory perception is veridical or nonveridical, true or mistaken; as long as it is presented to you, it is regarded as the skandha of form. This seems to be a peculiarly Yogacarin notion.

FEELING-TONE

The second skandha is *vedana*, or *sor wa*, "feeling-tone," and is regarded as one of the most important psychophysical constituents. It is said that feeling-tone permeates all of our sensory perceptions, not just our ordinary mental processes. As soon as we perceive something through any of the sensory mediums there is already a feeling-tone involved. No sensory perception is free from the overtones of feeling. It is quite usual to regard sensory perceptions as something passive and mental processes as something active. They say that certain objects stimulate your sense organs and then your mind responds to that in an active way. The object operates on you by stimulating your senses. Feeling-tone therefore acts as the necessary condition for our indulgence in sensuality.

Sensory perceptions are not passive but active in the sense that as soon as we perceive something, there is some overtone of feeling involved in that experience. Due to the substratum of awareness these experiences accumulate. As people often say, "once bitten, twice shy." If you had a particular experience in the past, as soon as you perceive a similar situation you are back in that past. Even if you don't exercise any intellectual power there is still some feeling-tone involved. You might feel nausea, you might feel fear, but there is an immediate reaction. It might be instinctive but nevertheless there is some feeling-tone associated with that whole situation.

An interesting thing here is that in the *Abhidharmasamuccaya* feeling is not interpreted as our normal notion of pleasure and pain, but in relation to the Yogacarin contention about traces and dispositions. From this point of view not everything is regarded as feeling. Traces and dispositions are provoked by certain situations and then we go through certain resultant experiences. The experiences we go through as a result of the actualization of traces and dispositions are called feeling-tones. It is said that if the traces and dispositions happen to be positive and healthy, the feelings that accompany that experience would also be positive and healthy. If the traces and dispositions happen to be negative, the experience we go through would also be negative as well. There is some homogeneous continuity between the potential and the actual.

Yogacara criticizes early Buddhists for saying that all the neutral feeling-tones we have—feelings that are without pleasure or pain—come from the accumulation of good karma or from healthy traces and dispositions. Yogacarins say that while neutrality is an aspect of the substratum of awareness it has nothing to do with the resultant experience of traces and dispositions, because as soon as there is any manifestation of karma it is no longer neutral; it has already assumed some kind of determination. Buddhism normally regards any type of feeling as vedana or feeling-tone. The Yogacarins claimed that feeling-tone really refers to any experience that we have as the result of past karma or past traces and dispositions. Other Buddhists claim that a neutral feeling-tone is also a feeling, but the Yogacarins denied this and claimed that it was impossible to have a neutral feeling. Neutrality is part of the substratum of awareness. It is not ethically or psychologically wholesome or unwholesome, while pleasure or pain arises as a result of our traces and dispositions. Feeling-tone is therefore defined as the result of our past traces and dispositions. In other words, feeling-tone comes about when the traces and dispositions are actualized.

Early Buddhists, especially the Vaibhasika, claimed there

is such a thing as neutral feeling and it comes from creating wholesome karma or wholesome traces and dispositions. Yogacarins said that is not true; you cannot have a neutral feeling-tone as a result of wholesome karma or wholesome traces and dispositions. The early Buddhists based their assessment on the belief that positive feeling goes along with passion, negative feeling goes with aggression and neutral feeling goes with ignorance. When we take pleasure in certain things some positive feeling would be involved, when you have aggression and want to push things away, you accumulate negative situations, and when you don't do anything you are not creating any karma and that comes from ignorance. They explain it by relying on the standard Buddhist notion of the three poisons: passion, aggression, and ignorance. But Yogacarins would say that if you are passionate or aggressive you are already ignorant anyway so you don't have to be neutral to suffer from ignorance.

There is actually no such thing as indifference in this particular context because "neutral feeling" is not regarded as neutral at all. It depends upon what you are being indifferent about. If you are being indifferent because you are trying to be cool and to ignore the whole situation or because something is too insignificant for you to pay attention to some motive is involved. You cannot be indifferent without a motive. As long as there is some motive behind your response, it is already a result of your traces and dispositions. That motive has arisen for certain reasons. If there is a reason, you must have a feeling about it. The reason comes from your habitual tendencies and those habitual tendencies exist because of your traces and dispositions. It could arise from ignorance, but you could have also made a decision not to pay attention to something for a reason. It could be a clever tactic to escape some kind of trouble or to pretend you are not really aware of what you are doing. It would depend upon the situation.

The Yogacara system also divides the skandha of feeling into two types. The first is the mundane feeling in ordinary situations called "feeling-tone with sign" or feeling-tone with referent because there is some reference point. That feeling-tone is associated with all kinds of emotional instabilities. The second is the feeling-tone of advanced practitioners, called "feeling-tone without sign" or without a referent. These practitioners experience certain things but the feeling-tone involved with that is not associated with any embellishment as far as their psychological makeup is concerned. So there is feeling-tone with sign and feeling-tone without sign.

Feeling-tone with sign means "having some kind of strong, obsessive concern." It is the dualistic situation of having a feeling and then getting obsessively concerned with what your feeling is about. The focus of your feeling is the objective aspect and the feeling itself is the subjective aspect. That kind of obsessive concern has some referent. The meditator's feeling-tones have less demarcation between the feeling itself and what the meditator has a feeling about. The first type of feeling-tone involves *atma-bhava*, which is a kind of "egocentricity" (*dag zin* in Tibetan). The meditator's feeling-tone is free from that. That seems to be the distinction.

What's suggested here is that the five skandhas are not to be regarded as bad or something to be dismissed but as something you can learn to manage properly as you begin to progress. When Buddhists say, "There is no soul, only the five skandhas," you may take that to mean that if there is only the situation of five skandhas they need to be dismissed but that is not what the Yogacarins are saying. The only thing we are trying to change is the traces and dispositions. The medium remains the same in many ways and the medium is the five skandhas. The five skandhas really do not change.

The reason that our perception, conception, and so on are deluded is because of the traces and dispositions. The medium is the same in that you will still use your eyes to see and your nose to smell. You will still have five skandhas. Nonetheless, even though the medium is the same the contents will really be different.

PERCEPTION

The third skandha is *samjna* or *du she* or "perception," that particular mental process where the conscious operation begins to become selective. Certain things are taken in while other things are left out. Some kind of editing process is taking place. If we direct our attention to a particular object, we don't mistake that object for something else. There is clearly defined perception taking place. For example if we are in a noisy place, we don't get distracted but can draw our attention to a particular sensory object. It is said that the third psychophysical constituent has the function of making a proper assessment of the outside sensory inputs as well as making a proper assessment of and giving some order to the mental processes. Our thoughts and perceptions are ordered rather than chaotic. That orderliness comes from the third psychophysical constituent.

This aspect of mental activity is divided into mundane and supramundane levels. It is said the more we discover about our own basic psychological tendencies through meditation the more we will make a proper assessment of perception. On the mundane level, it means making a proper judgment of a particular situation, but on the supramundane or on the spiritual level, it means being aware of what is unwholesome and what is unwholesome as far as our psychological tendencies are concerned. That sort of proper judgment is performed through this particular mental activity. Perception therefore acts as the necessary condition for our engagement in wrong philosophical views and mistaken intellectual activities.

CONCEPTION

The fourth skandha is known as *samskara* or *dub ye* which is "conception," which on reflection may not be such a good translation. Conception has the function of directing our mind to a particular object and taking interest in that object.

The explanation for this skandha is that its function is to direct our mind to a particular object. It also has the ability to stimulate or provoke our traces and dispositions so that they compel or propel us to act. Maybe "drive" or "dispositions" or something of that sort would be a better translation. There is some kind of intention here; our conscious experience is intentional. Conception is not a habitual process. Its function is to direct our attention to a particular object. If we have a thought, that thought is about something. If we "will" something, there is something that is willed. Every single mental process has some directionality of its own. Conception or drive is a necessary condition for all the other skandhas to exist. The others skandhas only operate and are actualized through this fourth skandha because it propels them to direct themselves to a particular project.

What is consciousness? *Consciousness* means "being conscious of something," so every conscious act has a direction of some sort. There are two types of situations: we can direct our attention to a physical object or we can direct it to our mental processes. Sometimes we catch ourselves thinking about thinking something. That is the ability to direct your consciousness onto your own conscious procedure. If you are thinking something, you can direct your thinking to that thought. You can do that. There is the thought that is thinking about the thought, there is the thought that is being thought about, and there is the thinking process itself. This takes place with outside situations as well. There is always a split between the act and the object acted upon. This is the function of the fourth skandha. In other words, any conscious process has to be conscious of something. You cannot be conscious and not be conscious of something.

That is one aspect of the fourth skandha. The other aspect is that this skandha doesn't just direct your mind toward a particular object; it prepares you to act on situations. You do not just sit back; there is a need to act in certain situations. Without control over a situation we act quite instinctively.

That takes place because of the fourth skandha. There are these two types of operation for the fourth skandha. The first is just the ordinary situation where we are aware of certain things—there is the act of awareness and something to be aware of, and there is the act of feeling and something to be felt. The second is that when you have a particular feeling-tone or perception, you are compelled to act in a certain way through the guidance of that feeling-tone or perception. That act would be performed through the impetus of the fourth skandha. It is more like a "drive" than "conception." You might think you are acting instinctively but it would not necessarily be instinctive. Your actions would be associated with your traces and dispositions.

Drive can be divided into mundane and supra-mundane levels. On the mundane level, drive propels us to accumulate bad karma and engage in all kinds of harmful activities. On the supramundane level it can become the impetus to practice and advance on the path. As you begin to develop spiritually there could be an intelligent drive as well. You might act in a particular way, but that would not be drive in the ordinary sense because you are not being driven by your whims. It is an intelligent way of acting. In that case, it is not necessarily drive but there is still the need to act properly, on the spot. It is not that drive is present on the mundane level and absent on the supramundane level; it continues in a different form.

The fourth skandha drags your mind to a particular sensory object that really interests you, whatever it may be. That very ability to direct your mind *is* the fourth skandha; there is no fourth skandha apart from that. The act itself is the fourth skandha. In other words, the fourth skandha doesn't do that; the doing itself is the fourth skandha.

EMPIRICAL CONSCIOUSNESS

The fifth skandha is *vijnana* or *namshe*, which is "empirical consciousness," which we talked about earlier in terms of the three levels of consciousness. This last level of consciousness—empirical consciousness (*pravrtti-vijnana*)—is identical with the skandha of empirical consciousness (*vijnana*). This skandha is related to the five sense organs. If we look at the five skandhas in the context of the three levels of consciousness: the skandhas of feeling-tone, perception, and conception come under the heading of egocentric mentation, while the body (the skandha of form) and the last level of consciousness (the skandha of empirical consciousness) stem from the substratum of awareness. As we can see, egocentric mentation manifests in different ways through the five skandhas.

MIND AND MENTAL EVENTS

To understand empirical consciousness we need to discuss the way that the sensory perceptions relate to mind (*sem*) and mental events (*sem chung*). We also need to explore how mind and mental events relate to each other, for that seems to be an important issue here. The fundamental distinction in Yogacara philosophy between mind and mental events is that mind apprehends an object as a whole whereas mental events apprehend an object in its particulars. When we perceive a table, the perception of the table is related to mind, while the particular characteristics of that table are the object of perception for mental events. First we have an immediate perception of the table, and then we have certain feeling-tones and judgments involved with that particular perception. The immediate perception is the only thing that relates to mind. That seems to be the major distinction between the mind and mental events.

Mind and mental events cause each other and the causal relationship between the two exists continuously. That is why Asanga says, "We cannot literally say mind and mental events come into being simultaneously." Otherwise the mind wouldn't be able to create certain situations or act on mental events and mental events wouldn't be able to invoke certain situations. That causal relationship exists because in any mental act there is some time lag or interval between the two; between the mind's apprehension and the mental event. It would just be a matter of a fraction of a second, so we don't notice it. We might just become immediately aware of a color and a shape. We do not know what it is, then we begin to realize what it is, and on further reflection we can verify our experience through some kind of experiment.

We can take the classic Buddhist example of a rope and snake. First you see this elongated thing with some colored patches lying on the road and you think it's a snake. If you perform some further reflection, you might be able to verify what it actually is and say, "This is not a snake at all, it's a rope." All those mental events take place as a result of your immediate experience of that type of physical sensation. At no time is there just mind without mental events. That's what we mean by saying that mind and mental events are closely related with each other.

Whatever experience we have, it would be associated with a certain type of mental event, whether it be healthy, unhealthy, or neutral. Unhealthy situations exist due to certain mental events. Mental events are what actually create the traces and dispositions. Mental events take place and leave certain impressions on the substratum of awareness, which in turn arise again to create further mental events. The whole process continues this way. Mind and mental events are really temporary or momentary. Sometimes we visually experience something and then aurally experience something else, almost simultaneously. However there is some temporal order that we cannot detect in ordinary situations. Nonetheless that sort of situation exists. Anything we experience will leave some impression behind on the substratum and that creates the necessary condition for us to have further experiences of that sort in the future.

The way it is set out in the *Abhidharmasamuccaya*, mental events relate to the way we act in different situations in an unwholesome way, so that we defeat the whole purpose of doing certain things. They also relate to how we could make a proper assessment of a situation and act in ways that enable us to develop in a psychologically wholesome way. This is a description of how the mind operates as far as Yogacara philosophy is concerned. We have not yet discussed neuroses; how we act neurotically or how we act in a healthy way in certain situations. Those things are associated with certain mental events. We will discuss that in conjunction with the Buddhist path in the following chapters and then go on to how the mind is transformed when we attain enlightenment.

CONDITIONS OF COMPATIBILITY

As we have seen, we cannot say mind and mental events are totally identical or that they each maintain their own individuality, because they are closely related to one another. There are binding factors in that situation and these are known as conditions of compatibility (*tsung den*). There are said to be five conditions of compatibility.

Compatibility of the sensory organ: if mind is involved with the visual organ, the mental events (feelings, perception, or whatever they may be) would also be involved with the visual organ. Compatibility exists between the mind and the mental events. We will be going into great detail about mental events in later chapters so at this stage we don't have to bother with the details.

Compatibility of the sensory object: if the mind directs its attention to a particular object, the mental events would also be connected with that object. If the mind has directed its attention to a table, the mental events would not be about something else but would also be involved with that perception.

Compatibility of appearance: if mind perceives a particular object to be blue, all the mental events (feelings, perceptions and so on) would receive similar information. The difference between this and the former factor and that appearance can sometimes be delusive but you cannot be mistaken about the object. You could think that something looks blue but it might not be blue at all. On further reflection, you might find out it is yellow. Even when you have that kind of illusory perception the mind and mental events have still received the same kind of information. On the other hand, if you see a table it is a table, you cannot be mistaken about that. That seems to be the distinction.

Compatibility of time: whenever there is some primary mental act there is also a mental event associated with that act so they take place at the same time. They are copresent, as they say. They are present at the same time.

Compatibility of substance: mind and mental events are made up of the same stuff. There is no distinction between the two on the substantial level.

These are the five conditions of compatibility that link or bridge the gap between mind and mental events. We need to investigate and explore this further. For instance, when it is said that mind apprehends the object in its entirety, what does this mean? What does it mean to say mental events apprehend only the parts?

We cannot say mind only apprehends the whole and mental event only apprehend the parts. There must be some kind of overlap between the two. If there were no overlap between the two, there would be no communication between the mind and mental events and we would have a fragmented perception of the world. There must be some kind of overlap. This distinction is based on the primary function of each of these mental processes. The mind and mental events apprehend the same object but they have different functions. Because they apprehend the same object, there is some relationship between the two, some kind of overlapping situation. The mind's apprehension is totally nonconceptual; it is immediate perception of the object. Mental events are conceptual. All feeling-tones and judgmental processes are related to mental events, rather than to the primary mental act of perception.

Compatibility of time should also be clarified. It is said

we should not take this literally, that mind and mental events are both present at the same time and in the same space. However, no two things can occupy the same space and time; there has to be some logical or chronological order. If they are copresent in the literal sense, there would be no chronological or logical order, and that would violate causal law. The mind has to operate on the mental event and the mental events have to react to the mind so there has to be some interaction between the two. Interaction naturally implies a causal relationship and causality cannot exist unless there is temporal sequence. Cause has to precede effect and effect has to follow cause. The reason it is said that mind and mental events are copresent is that they are copresent in the ordinary sense of the word rather than in a strict logical sense. It does not mean that the mind and mental events occupy the same point in space and time.

Asanga, the master who wrote the *Abhidharmasamuccaya*, argues that while some Buddhist masters maintain that the copresence of mind and mental events means they literally happen simultaneously, all kinds of difficulties will arise if we believe that. These masters use the examples of the flame of a lamp and its shadow or two sticks leaning on each other to argue that one does not precede the other. Those examples are not quite relevant. Two sticks do not occupy the same space, they occupy different spaces, and a lamp first has to be lit before its shadow can come along, so there is a temporal sequence. Asanga says that such examples are very shallow on that level. When the *Abhidharmasamuccaya* talks about the copresence of mind and mental events, it is not saying there is no causal relationship. It just means the interval between cause and effect is so negligible they are almost copresent. Nonetheless, we should not get carried away by that and say they are literally copresent. When the mind and mental events are said to be made out of the same substance, we again have to make some provisions for this. It does not literally mean mind and mental events are made out of the same substance, it just means there is a homogeneous relationship between them. There is resemblance between the two but they are not literally identical. The mind and the mental events cannot be identified as the same entity.

If we identify the mind with mental events we run into all kinds of difficulties. By and large, Buddhists have rejected what is known as the "cause and effect identity theory," which says that while cause and effect are seen in different ways, from an objective point of view they are the same thing. Buddhists say that the only continuity that exists between cause and effect is a homogeneous relationship. They are not literally made of the same substance and there is no real identity. Like milk and cream, there is a homogeneous relationship, but we cannot say that milk is cream. In a similar way, there is a homogenous relationship between mind and mental effects but the mind is not the mental events. It should be noted these discussions arose as a reaction to the beliefs of some of the Hindu schools. For example, a Hindu school known as Samkhya says there is no distinction between cause and effect. Buddhists rejected that notion.

In terms of our perception of the world, five conditions of compatibility exist between the mind and mental events. It is said that as far as our perception of the world is concerned they are the necessary ground for having any kind of perception. The *Abhidharmasamuccaya* makes it clear that we cannot maintain these conditions in a pedantic way and that some provisions have to be made for exceptional cases and so on. Generally, the mind and mental events are somewhat distinct, but they also interact and are intimately related with one another. That intimate relationship forms a complex system if you like, in terms of understanding the world. We will discuss what the mental events are in the following chapters, because they are more related to spiritual and ethical issues than to psychological and philosophical ones.

That seems to be the functions of the different skandhas. As we go along we will refer to these skandhas so having a general understanding of them will be helpful for following the discussion. The order of the five skandhas is not really an indication of a particular chronological order. They are really simultaneous. In some ways the fourth skandha would be first if you want to look at the whole thing chronologically because there is some kind of directedness to our conscious procedure in anything we experience. If we feel something, feeling-tone is directed toward a particular object. If we perceive something, perception is directed toward a particular object, and so on. It happens on all levels. On the sensory level, there is the act of seeing and then there is what is seen. There is always a conscious act and an object that is acted upon. The conscious act is always directed toward something so it is a necessary condition for all the skandhas except form. Form is not mental so it cannot direct itself toward anything. But whenever a conscious act is involved, there is some kind of directionality, so the fourth skandha is the necessary condition for all the others. In some ways it precedes all the others.

QUESTIONS

QUESTION: What happens at the time of death when you haven't got a body? How does not having a skandha of form affect the rest of the skandhas?

RINPOCHE: During the death process we withdraw from all of the skandhas except for the empirical consciousness. The skandhas begin to diminish and gradually lose their efficacy. After the death process they manifest again in the bardo state. It is only due to physical changes that they diminish and that diminishment brings about certain states of consciousness. However after the death process consciousness begins to regain its power. If we look at the texts on death and dying, they say consciousness goes through some changes but then regains its power. All you have is consciousness; there is no body there. Sometimes it's called the "subtle body" but the subtle body is not really a body. It's a mistaken notion of a heavenly body of some sort. Some people have a near-death experience and when revived say they thought they had a body but when they stumbled over something they didn't knock it over and were really surprised. That means it is only the illusion of having a body rather than having any concrete body as such.

QUESTION: Is egocentric consciousness present during death?

RINPOCHE: Yes, but egocentric mentation has fewer efficacies at that time than in ordinary situations during life. It is said that due to the lack of efficacy of egocentric mentation we can actually attain enlightenment during the bardo state if we are able to become conscious of what is happening. Nonetheless egocentric mentation is still present.

QUESTION: I have seen the first skandha described as a basic flash of panic that asks, "Do I exist or not?" Then the other skandhas are said to follow on from that panic in order to reinforce the notion "I exist." How does that fit in with our physical form?

RINPOCHE: You acquire physical form due to that panic. If we look at it in that context, panic starts on the level of the substratum of awareness. At that stage you would not be conscious of yourself as an individual person. However once that type of consciousness begins to take place, you wonder what's happening and because of that the need to assume a body arises. In a way, the five skandhas develop along with the three levels of consciousness. They develop at the same time.

QUESTION: You said that conception or samskara has the function of directing the mind to an object. Could you give an example of directing the mind to interest in an object?

RINPOCHE: You are directing your interest onto me now. It is due to conception that you are able to direct your attention to what I am saying. Other functions are also involved, but it is conception that enables you to direct your attention to certain things and take an interest on that level. There is some kind of directionality. It took a long time for Western psychologists to find out there is such a thing as intentionality of mind. It had to wait for Edmond Husserl to come along in Germany to say, "There is such a thing as intentionality of mind." But yes, it's a mental process and the function of conception is to be able to direct the mind to a particular thing. You have a thought and then there is what the thought is about. Whenever you are thinking something your mind is directed toward something. During sleep that intentionality takes place on the inner conscious level as well as on the outer physical level. We are able to direct our attention to physical objects and we are also able to direct our consciousness toward the conscious process itself. In some sense this is why we are able to dream. There are all kinds of things happening and then there is a spectator who is watching the whole thing. There is a kind of split in some sense.

QUESTION: If you are in a situation where you don't feel pleasure or pain are you really feeling one or the other and just not recognizing it? Should one investigate those situations?

RINPOCHE: Yes, that is precisely what we are talking about. It's not good enough to say, "This is what the Yogacarins say, maybe it's true and maybe it's not." We have to reflect on the whole situation and see whether it is true or not. We have to look at how we respond to different situations and then see whether these processes take place or not and then look at how you feel about it. Some kind of reflection is necessary. Most of the time our indifferent will have some kind of negative connotation, there is not enough interest involved. Equilibrium might mean that you are trying not to be biased or preventing your emotional overtones from coloring your perception of a situation. It would have positive overtones. It would be a good thing karmically because it would leave positive traces and dispositions. It is a karmic process on that level. If you attain enlightenment, there could be some level of equilibrium totally free from karmic tendencies because you would not leave any traces and dispositions behind.

QUESTION: The Reichian School of Western psychology says the body imprisons feelings in a physical sense and that to be psychologically healthy we have to break through the armor that imprisons our feelings and release them. How does that fit in with the relationship between body and the other skandhas involved in egocentric mentation?

RINPOCHE: I think that type of thinking goes back to Plato, maybe even earlier. The Greeks are responsible for thinking of the body as something that imprisons your soul. Descartes is responsible for that too. For the last two to three thousand years, Western psychologies and philosophies have struggled with this notion. It is called the problem of "the ghost in the machine." As far as Buddhists are concerned it is not necessarily a problem because Buddhists do not regard body and mind as two separate entities. There might be some relationship between the two. Due to the fact that body and mind are able to interact, the body is not viewed as something that entraps consciousness or the soul. Buddhists generally don't believe in a soul or view the body as something that has entrapped consciousness.

QUESTION: Would the Buddhist approach advocate or condone the purposeful release of feelings? In that type of therapy, you actualize these feelings by seeking them out and letting them go. You lie on the floor and scream your head off.

RINPOCHE: Buddhists would look at that as useful if it is done in the right way. A Buddhist would also try to encourage a person to reflect on the whole situation and not just think, "Now I've got that off my chest, I don't have to worry about it for the next couple of months" or "If something happens, I can scream and get it done away with." It may be quite healthy to actualize your feelings in that way, but you still have to learn why something is happening instead of thinking, "It doesn't matter how it happened, so long as I can get it off my chest it will be okay." If whatever we do leaves some imprint on our mind, those imprints will coerce us into acting in a particular way, which in turn would leave more imprints. We have to somehow break that chain reaction.

QUESTION: But it could be seen as exhausting karma?

RINPOCHE: Yes, in a way, because that person would not hang onto those things for a while, which is pretty healthy. Otherwise that person might become increasingly negative or more and more desperate and develop a tremendous amount of unhealthy attitudes.

QUESTION: If you say there is no indifference, we are always looking at things with some idea of a threat or a promise. Where does that sense of threat come from?

RINPOCHE: That type of feeling comes from the dualistic notion of "me" and "other." On top of that, it is about our desire to nurture and nourish our own egocentricity.

QUESTION: How did the other schools that weren't Yogacarin handle that primal hope and fear?

RINPOCHE: They would also go along with this explanation except they would say there is such a thing as neutral feeling. Sometimes you're just there without accumulating either good karma or bad karma. To put it simply, you just sit there, but that state of mind comes from good karma that you have accumulated in the past.

QUESTION: Do Yogacarins say you accumulate some karma no matter what you do?

RINPOCHE: You do not accumulate karma in a state where you are not doing anything. Our whole conscious process is movement. It's always doing one thing or another. It's not really at rest until we begin to work through the habitual process. If we are able to work through that we might be able to be in a state where we don't perform any mental act that would bring about wholesome or unwholesome results.

QUESTION: Is there any possibility of seeing beyond the level of pleasure and pain before we attain enlightenment?

RINPOCHE: There is a possibility of seeing a break between those two situations. That is what meditation is for really. We might be able to see some kind of gap in our thought processes. In a similar way all the other mental activities would have some kind of gap somewhere. We might have glimpses of certain breaks in our habitual patterns. We can't experience it properly unless we have worked through it properly. There is experience, but still it might be colored by your emotions. Meditation would make it more and more possible for you to work through that. That gap would not be a neutral feeling as we understand it either. Meditation is not supposed to numb you so that you can't feel either pain or pleasure. It is supposed to lead you beyond feeling all three types of feelings in some sense. The third feeling is related to the other two anyway. There is the possibility for the gap that you experience in meditation to be something beyond what you might experience in ordinary circumstances.

QUESTION: All the experiences we are talking about—the actualization of the vasanas and feeling experiences—are all outflows. How do you practice non-outflow in meditation?

RINPOCHE: That is what we normally try to do. Theravada meditation says, "Whatever thought comes up, label it as 'just thought'." You try to not see it with any kind of overtone, which is being nonjudgmental. What they are saying is that if you have an aggressive thought in meditation, you don't have to jump up and wash out your mouth because you have discovered you are not a proper vessel for meditation. You just see it as a thought. Meditative techniques in all Buddhist traditions are geared toward that.

QUESTION: What constitutes karma?

RINPOCHE: *Samskaras* or "habitual patterns." According to

Yogacara, the *vasanas* or "traces and dispositions" are retained in the substratum and when the appropriate circumstance arises they are stimulated and become actualized. They get actualized in action, which makes karma. It's a vicious circle. The more you act and actualize your vasanas, the more traces and dispositions are left behind because of that act. The ability to arrest this cycle comes from meditation. You try to be mindful and aware in all daily situations so that you do not act instinctively. You start to see why you are responding in certain ways. Otherwise you will get more and more mired in habitual situations. Sometimes we think we know certain things or we intuit certain situations and we might be correct. But sometimes habitual process becomes so ingrained in us; we may only think we are intuiting something when we are simply acting instinctively because we have become so proficient at our habitual way of responding.

QUESTION: Do we make karma with our intention? It would be very important to guard or know your intention when you are responding to a situation.

RINPOCHE: Conception is normally colored by feelings—either wholesome or unwholesome—so that whenever we intend something there is always a feeling-tone involved. However, it does not necessarily have to be that way. If you get enlightened, you would still direct your intention toward certain things but it would not be colored by your subjective feelings. That doesn't mean you become insensitive.

QUESTION: I always thought that karma means "motivation and intention" and that is what really starts off the vicious cycle of karma.

RINPOCHE: Intention doesn't necessarily have to be present all the time to create karma. We create karma in other ways too. We don't necessarily premeditate a lot of our actions but premeditated actions are even more disastrous karmically. The law of jurisprudence operates on a similar principle. Sometimes you do certain things without intention and still get prosecuted, but if you do something with intention, you are going to really get it. It's a similar kind of thing with karma. Karma is heavier if something is done with motivation.

QUESTION: Is there such a thing as unintentional karma? If everything arises from the mind, even at a subtle level, then intention must exist.

RINPOCHE: It depends upon how we define *intention*. If we mean "premeditated action," it doesn't have to be like that, but traces and dispositions would still coerce us in an unconscious way. There is some kind of intention involved on an unconscious level. However it is hard to define properly. Psychoanalysts say the things we do unconsciously are actually decisions we make unconsciously. So I think it really depends. If we try to formulate the Buddhist definition of *intention* it would normally mean "premeditated act." Things without intention also bring about certain results but they are not as heavy. That's another thing, as far as Buddhists are concerned, there is no pre-established rule that says doing something will automatically mean you are going to get punished. The degree of prosecution will depend on your act, but the prosecution is not meted out by anyone, it is of your own making.

QUESTION: Is the mundane level feeling-tone just some sort of editing process?

RINPOCHE: No, feeling-tone does not involve any editing process. If you get an electric shock you don't edit it, you just happen to be in that situation and you get a buzz. The editing process takes place on the skandha of perception. You could be in a noisy situation so you select certain sounds and leave others out. There may be all kinds of things in your visual field but you can look at one object and leave the rest out. You can direct your attention to a particular smell and not smell the others. That sort of thing takes place on all kinds of levels. Feeling-tone, on the other hand, is very immediate, which means that as far as your experience goes there is no interpretation involved. On the perceptual level there can be some kind of interpretation so that what you experience might not be what you actually experience in a strict sense. There could be some subjective interpretation involved there.

QUESTION: Does the substratum of awareness give rise to feeling-tone?

RINPOCHE: Yes, that's right. You might experience a phobia, for example, where your fear might be due to certain past associations. All of these things are actually associated with the substratum. Whatever we experience is dependent upon the substratum, including the fourth skandha, which is the ground for the operation of all the other skandhas. You become less and less subject to the influence of the substratum as you progress with your practice. Still you could have feeling-tones without having the substratum because there are two levels of feeling-tones. When it is said that you work through all your emotional instabilities and attain enlightenment, people imagine this means you become really numb because you no longer experience emotions. However there could still be feeling-tones involved but they do not impact on your mind so that traces and dispositions are left behind to become actualized at some later time. They are subjective from the point of view that there is a subject to experience them but it is not egocentric. There is a distinction between the two. As long as there is a feeling that feeling must belong to a particular individual. You cannot have a feeling without an individual. But normally there is always some overly obsessive concern with the whole situation. When that is worked through, the feeling-tone is still owned by a particular individual, but that individual is not obsessed with it.

QUESTION: We have such preconceptions about ordinary things. If something you are familiar with gives you a real shock, how would you relate to that?

RINPOCHE: You either discover a completely new dimension of your consciousness or you could lose your ground completely. There is no reference as far as your past experiences are concerned, so that experience might produce paranoia, in which case you will freak out. But at the same time, there is the possibility of exploring another dimension of your consciousness.

QUESTION: As you progress with your meditation and experience a less dualistic situation is there less perception or less editing?

RINPOCHE: They work together all the time in ordinary circumstances and in some ways they work on a higher level too. On a higher level there is still discriminating ability but the discrimination does not get things mixed up. It does not do as much siding with certain situations while ignoring others, which is what happens in ordinary circumstances. You still have the ability to distinguish one thing from another. You use judgment, but that judgment is to the point, it is not charged with emotional biases. You are able to make a proper assessment of the situation. We can develop that type of perception into *prajna* or "discriminating awareness." You still have a tremendous ability to discriminate but that discrimination is not the type of discrimination we are familiar with; racial discrimination or ordinary discrimination between a cup of tea and a cup of coffee. You are able to make a proper assessment of a situation without getting bogged down by your past experiences. The less you are influenced by past experiences the more you are able to make a proper assessment of a situation.

QUESTION: Does dualistic mean separate?

RINPOCHE: When Buddhists talk about nondualism, they do not mean "everything is one," where subject and object become one in a numerical sense. It does not mean "oneness" where suddenly you discover there is this gigantic whole that you happen to be part of. It is not a question of how things are; it is more a question of how you view things. The less you view things in a dualistic way, the more you are able to make a proper judgment, because you are freed from your own preconceptions. But that does not lead you to becoming one with things. You are not bringing two things together and making them into one object. To put it more technically, philosophers say it is an epistemological issue, because it deals with knowledge, rather than an ontological question that deals with things as they are or the way things exist.

QUESTION: When you purify intentionality is that called "the unintentional activity of someone who is enlightened?"

RINPOCHE: Buddhas also act according to situations. It is not as if buddhas do not make assessments of certain situations and then act accordingly. They do. Their need to act would be somewhat different from the way ordinary people act, which is due to the influence of traces and dispositions. The fourth skandha provides the impetus for ordinary people to act that way. Enlightened beings would act but their actions would be more spontaneous. Nonetheless, they still have the need to act. An enlightened being does not just perform an act arbitrarily. An enlightened being would act in a certain way in a certain situation and not act that way in other situations. There is some difference.

QUESTION: Does a buddha have five skandhas?

RINPOCHE: Yes. Why not?

QUESTION: The Yogacara point of view says a buddha has five skandhas. What about the Madhyamaka point of view?

RINPOCHE: Yogacara, Madhyamaka, and the other mahayana schools would say a buddha does not have five skandhas in the ordinary sense because a buddha's perceptual skills get perfected and no longer function the way they ordinarily functioned. Nonetheless, five psychophysical constituents are involved. Early Buddhists believed that buddhas do have psychophysical constituents. Not only that, they believed that the psychophysical constituents cannot be purified so that even buddhas suffer from them. They use the story of Buddha's brother firing a cannon at him and blowing a piece off his toe to show that Buddha was subject to that sort of thing and suffered from the psychophysical constituents. As far as the mahayana is concerned, Buddha had five skandhas, but his management of them was totally different to ordinary people. That's all. They do not necessarily mean Buddha was immutable, that his body is so solid nothing can blow it up.

QUESTION: If an enlightened being does not have any traces and dispositions where is the ground for them to act correctly?

RINPOCHE: Due to the sharpening of perception you begin to develop prajna. This sharpening of discriminating awareness takes place so that you are able to make a proper judgment that is not for or against anything. Normally, when we make a judgment, we evaluate the situation and make a decision that involves for and against. When an enlightened being makes a judgment it is not for or against. It is about seeing what the situation demands it and then that is done.

QUESTION: If there is an increase in a person's ability to act correctly does that mean it's irrelevant how another person experiences that action?

RINPOCHE: No, it is not irrelevant. That's the thing. An enlightened person is able to make a judgment that is proper for the other person as well. Sometimes the other person might not see it as proper or wholesome, but in time that person might discover that what has been done has been really good in the long run. Responsibility is there but not as a burden of some sort. Normally, when we feel responsible, we feel completely bogged down. The more responsibility we feel, the more bogged down we get. Enlightened beings might feel responsible. They might act in certain situations, but they would not get bogged down by their responsibilities because it is not a decision for or against. It is about making a proper assessment of the immediate situation, rather than conceptually elaborating on the whole thing and creating a different picture altogether, as we normally do. The act might be the same as any other person but the intention would be different. If there were to be a nuclear holocaust and someone had the ability to stop it, there might not be any difference between the way an ordinary person does it and the way an enlightened being does it, but the intention would be quite different. It is the mental attitude involved that makes the difference. It's not so much how the act is carried out. How the act is carried out might be the same, as much as enlightened beings would eat food and that sort of thing.

QUESTION: Isn't the underlying principle of an enlightened being's action to benefit all sentient beings?

RINPOCHE: Yes but an enlightened person might not be too concerned about that either. You might not necessarily feel obsessed with helping others. Enlightened beings are really supposed to act in accordance with a situation as it arises. When a bodhisattva—someone who adopts the mahayana attitude—tries to practice, he or she might make mistakes. Something he or she thinks is beneficial for others might turn out to be unbeneficial. But as you develop, whatever you engage in becomes more and more precise and accurate.

QUESTION: You get very contradictory stories about the Buddha. There was someone who was running after the Buddha trying to kill him, but the more he ran, the more the Buddha kept at the same distance. Yet the same Buddha had to suffer through dysentery.

RINPOCHE: Early Buddhists depict Buddha as being an ordinary human being. He had mental perfection but he was a human being subject to certain situations. He had more skills than others, but that did not exclude him from being a human being. In the Buddhist tradition there are certain parables called the *Jataka Tales*, which were written for lay people. Lay people want to believe in all kinds of stories. That is the way they practice. But sometimes a psychological interpretation is given to those stories. This especially happens in the mahayana tradition. The stories would not necessarily be historical facts. I think early Buddhists would have taken them to be more literal than later Buddhists. Later Buddhists tend to give a psychological interpretation to almost everything that takes place for certain individuals. Historically it is devastating, but individually, I think it's very good, because you begin to really understand what the whole thing is all about. It serves two purposes. Lay people, who do not want to inquire further into the doctrinal side, can just have these fantastic stories about the buddhas and bodhisattvas and they can practice that way. Someone who is more interested could learn further and see how all those things can be interpreted. For example, just before the Buddha attained enlightenment, demons sent their daughters to tempt Buddha. Psychologically interpreted, that means Buddha completely overcame passion and aggression simultaneously on the spot. All these internal neurotic tendencies were completely cut through and ever since then he was free from them. It doesn't literally mean that all these emanations rolled up. *The Life and Liberation of Padmasambhava* is another really good example of how you could interpret a life story in two ways; one for lay people and one for practitioners.

QUESTION: If you say to yourself, "If I veer from this path, put me back on," would situations arise by themselves to put you back on the path?

RINPOCHE: That is possible, because if you really commit yourself to practice, it is an ongoing pursuit. Even when you think you have given yourself a break, you really have not, because the break becomes part of the process. You begin to realize that the break wasn't a break at all. It is an error and correction procedure that goes on all the time. Once you have committed yourself, that's it. There is no stopping.

QUESTION: Is it possible to become enlightened or to seek enlightenment without identifying yourself as a Buddhist or a follower of a particular path?

RINPOCHE: If you want to transcend being a Buddhist, first you need to become a Buddhist. Seriously; that is really a prerequisite for any spiritual practice in some ways. Once you get to the other side, it doesn't matter. You don't have to call yourself Buddhist or anything of the sort. But to be able to get there, you have to be Buddhist.

QUESTION: People follow the Christian path or the Hindu path and become enlightened through that process as well. Is it possible to not follow any particular system or scheme but just get lucky?

RINPOCHE: There is no luck. You are already unlucky, in some sense. Anyone who thinks that way, it will really become a problem for them at some stage. You do not have to be dogmatic about your practice, thinking that what you are doing is the answer to everything and what other people are doing is wrong, but a certain amount of commitment to a particular practice is necessary if you really want to progress spiritually. It does not matter what you are committing yourself to. You will not make any advancement otherwise. You might make it, but you will be doing it the hard way. To think that way is really not to take any step toward anything. Each tradition has certain intricacies and certain practices. It is not just a matter of calling yourself something or other. It is really a question of *you*. It is not about signing your name on the dotted line and becoming a club member. That is just external. As far as the spiritual side goes, it is a matter of life and death, in some sense. It is really personal on that level.

QUESTION: When we talk about commitment to the path, if

that's what you want to do, that's fine. But I find it absurd to do that with the goal of enlightenment in mind. It is not a question of when the train is going to arrive, it is just a question of the journey.

RINPOCHE: Once the train has left the station, it is obviously going to arrive somewhere. But I greatly approve of that approach; that is my own approach, anyway. Thinking about a destination does not get you there. You need to embark on the vehicle, and once you have embarked on the vehicle, you have already left for your destination. Thinking about the destination might only create a problem. You might want to get off at the next station, which could completely delay your journey. The incentive is just to embark on the path. Once you have embarked on the path, that's it. You have already done the research. You have looked at the map and know when a certain vehicle leaves from what station and reaches what destination. You have to do the research and you have to have enough money to take the journey. Once you have done that, you get into the vehicle, and that is it. If you think too much about the destination, about what it's going to be like and whether you will be able to support yourself once you get there, you could decide to get off and wander around somewhere else. You might finally end up going back, but you have wasted so much time. That seems to be the whole procedure. That is the whole Buddhist path: the hinayana, mahayana, and vajrayana. On the hinayana level, you do the research; you think about the goal, then you make the proper arrangements, and so on. On the mahayana level, the journey is already taking place and you no longer need to concern yourself too much about the destination.

QUESTION: What about ongoing doubt? You are saying we should trust in our training, trust in the vehicle, that what we are on is okay.

RINPOCHE: Occasional doubts are fine. They might keep you busy while you are there. They are like occasional sneezes. In some ways, that produces some sparks on the journey, which is not regarded as anything bad. But if you are too preoccupied with a goal situation, it could become a self-defeating process.

QUESTION: If the mind is immediate perception, is it samsaric or nonsamsaric?

RINPOCHE: Mind provides the ground for both samsara and nirvana. It is a necessary condition for enlightened beings as well as for deluded beings. Mind is quite indeterminate on that level. "Mind" here really means the eight levels of consciousness.

QUESTION: Would a feeling-tone only arise because you are looking at some object?

RINPOCHE: Yes, otherwise you would receive certain information due to your primary mental act and then receive other information through your mental events, but that does not happen. Whenever you have a particular experience there is some uniformity between the two. And most of the time we don't really notice it very much.

QUESTION: Are subsequent mental events colored by previous ones? Is every mental event that occurs become an extra facet to a subsequent mental event?

RINPOCHE: Due to our traces and dispositions that becomes more and more of a possible situation. If we accumulate certain traces and dispositions, we will continue to think and see certain things in that particular way due to the influence of those traces and dispositions.

QUESTION: If we can learn to discriminate between positive and negative mental events, can we begin to sort out what traces and dispositions we should absorb and what traces and dispositions we should avoid?

Rinpoche: Just by being able to detect which mental events are taking place and by being observant of them will create some possibility of avoiding that type of thing; that is a really important issue in Buddhist practice. Even if you are studying tantra, it is still really important to study the mind and mental events because most of the deities are really symbolic expressions of our psychological makeup. Sometimes deities wear five skulls as a crown. Unless you know what the five skulls symbolize, you would just think the Tibetans must be totally out of their minds. Maybe they produced all this weird art because they took hallucinogenic mushrooms. In tantric iconography, those five skulls represent the five skandhas. It is not as simple as that, but putting it simply, they represent the five skandhas. The deities also wear fifty-one human skulls as a rosary around their neck. The psychological implication here is that the fifty-one skulls represent the fifty-one mental events. These images are a method for transforming your mind and mental events through the repeated performance of visualization.

You begin to purify your perception by constantly performing that kind of visualization. The whole practice really involves being able to relate to healthy and unhealthy mental events so that you can understand how they relate to you and how they actually operate. We normally choose to ignore those things. We might not even make a distinction between mind and mental events. As far as I know this sort of distinction isn't really made in the West. Western thought tends to make three types of distinctions between mental acts: cognitive, conative, and affective. Cognitive has to do with knowledge, conative is related to action and the will, and affective has to do with the emotions. There is no detailed explanation about mental events as far as I know. For Buddhists, the mental events are really important. You are constantly reflecting on yourself, especially through meditation, because you have to learn more and more about how your mind is operating.

QUESTION: Wouldn't that keep you in samsara continuously?

RINPOCHE: No, I don't think so, it is not the fact of "what we are" that is keeping us in bondage, it is our mismanagement of the whole situation. What we are has nothing to do with being bound. Our wrong assessment of the situation has created our bondage. Mahayanists don't say you have to come to any kind of cessation on that level. The neuroses do not cease as much as they are seen for what they are. Not being able to see our own neuroses for what they are is what creates the neuroses; it is not a matter of having all these neuroses as an intrinsic thing and then suffering from them. Almost all Buddhist texts are laid out in a particular format, known as "ground, path, and fruition." That is the standard Buddhist way of approaching anything. Most of the time, ground is related to theoretical questions about Buddhism: where you start from, what you do, how you equip yourself to take the journey. The path is about how to take the journey. Finally you attain the goal. We have almost finished our discussion of the ground.

Relative and Absolute Truth

To understand what consciousness is all about in the context of Yogacara philosophy, we need to understand the classic Buddhist distinction between absolute and relative truth. The difference between the absolute and the relative is quite simple. Even within our normal experiences things sometimes appear to be other than what they really are. We might gain an impression about a particular person from observing his or her overt behavior and we might say, "So and so is gentle" or "So and so is clever," but we might have come to the wrong conclusion. Through further acquaintance, we might discover that the person we thought was clever is really a schmuck. We might look through a window and see an ice-cream but it turns out to be a clever plastic device. So, even in our normal experiences, there is this distinction between what something appears to be and what it really is.

These types of distinctions are also made on the level of consciousness. We have certain impressions about ourselves—about who we are and what we are—and we also have a deeper level of who we are and what we are. Buddhist philosophies generally tend to treat mind as something that is completely momentary, as a point-instant, without any duration and with no persisting history. According to the Yogacara however, mind can be divided into two different levels: it can be treated on the absolute level and also on the relative level.

BASIC AWARENESS

What is consciousness? When we talk about consciousness we are really talking about the eight levels of consciousness. But there is another level of mind. There is a state of basic awareness or wisdom that is free from these eight levels of consciousness. When we talk about consciousness on that level, it is a much more sophisticated experience; it is not our normal type of conscious experience.

It is said that the substratum of awareness is the basic ground upon which these two types of conscious experience exist. We have ordinary conscious experiences as well as the experience of wisdom. The wisdom aspect of consciousness and the ordinary aspect of consciousness are abstractions from the substratum of awareness. I don't know whether "abstraction" is a good word for it, maybe "extraction" is better. These two aspects rise simultaneously from the substratum of awareness. Neurosis and wisdom arise simultaneously. It's not that first you were quite clever and then you ate the apple and fell. The substratum of awareness contains both. We could either fall into our ordinary conception of ourselves, which amounts to the same thing as forgetting ourselves, or we could discover who we are and come in close contact with ourselves. Both situations arise out of the substratum of awareness.

The higher level of consciousness, called "basic awareness" or "wisdom," is the fundamental nature of our own mind. It is luminous and totally free from all kinds of neuroses and confusions and is called buddhanature. On the other hand, we have ordinary subjective experiences, which are subjected to all kinds of emotional imbalances. We should be aware that this explanation has some value in Buddhist tantra as well. Buddhist tantra places a great emphasis on luminosity and the basic freedom of the human mind. Yogacarins were the precursors of that view. Basic awareness cannot be regarded as personal property. We cannot say, "This is my wisdom and you can't have a slice of it." The basic nature of our own mind is all-pervading. It is something everybody possesses and something everyone can discover because it is intrinsic to our own being.

Yogacara philosophy placed a far greater emphasis on the luminosity aspect of mind than on our empirical experience of consciousness. The Yogacarins suggested that what we normally experience—our emotional imbalances, neuroses, and so on—are incidental, rather than intrinsic to, ourselves. Those things come about due to a wrong assessment of the whole situation due to our own ingrained habits. Once we undo our habits, we begin to discover the basic nature of our mind. It is totally luminous and free from neurotic embellishments. These two polar situations in our conscious experience are labeled "samsara" and "nirvana."

Samsara and nirvana, or bondage and freedom, are not explained in geographical terms. Nirvana is not some place you can go to. When the mind is freed from its own unnecessary paraphernalia it is able to discover its own basic being. Nirvana is one side of our consciousness and samsara is another so it is a matter of going from one aspect to the other. The reason we are unable to discover the luminosity aspect of the mind is because of our unconscious tendency to not acknowledge our own basic awareness. We take delight in being able to feel comfortable in the neurotic state and deny the freedom we possess.

PURE AND IMPURE STATES

It is said when we experience the eight levels of consciousness we are subject to an impure state: that is to impermanence, suffering, and selflessness. *Impure state* means that "our mind is completely embellished" and we experience all kinds of emotional instabilities. *Impermanence* means that "whatever we experience is momentary"; everything that we think of as permanent turns out to be impermanent. That experience leads to suffering. Whatever does not last creates tremendous suffering. That leads to selflessness. On the other hand, if we are able to discover our own basic being, that will lead to a state of purity. Our mind will be totally liberated from its own embellishments and emotional imbalances, which will lead to a permanent state. This means that whatever we experience is not impermanence as we normally experience it and does not produce suffering. There is a general sense of contentment or joy and that finally leads to the notion of a real self.

These views are quite interesting, in that Buddhists normally say quite the opposite. Yogacara philosophy turned to these notions and they also became quite important in tantra because there is a kind of transition from one state to the other in a well-defined manner. What it amounts to is this: when our mind is corrupted by all kinds of neuroses and emotional imbalances, we dwell in samsara, and once the corruptions are removed, we attain nirvana.

It is also said the substratum of awareness pervades our entire physical organism, which means the traces and dispositions are not totally mental. There are physical traces and dispositions, verbal traces and dispositions, and mental traces and dispositions. Any physical act we perform conditions our physical actions, any utterance we make condition our verbal activity, and any mental act we perform leaves its traces and dispositions on the mind. So there are three types of traces and dispositions. The substratum of awareness is understood to pervade the whole of our physical organism rather than just the brain in this way.

QUESTIONS

QUESTION: Could you go over that progression of impure state of impermanence, suffering, and selflessness?

RINPOCHE: Impure state really means we normally discover

ourselves to be quite neurotic. We have all kinds of problems, which leads to the discovery of impermanence. We happen to be neurotic because we want things to be permanent but they do not turn out that way, which leads to suffering. We begin to suffer because our expectations are completely shattered, which leads to loss of self, and in some sense, to selflessness. We begin to despair due to an identity crisis of some sort. The opposite of this is the state of purity. A pure state means that we begin to discover who we are. As there is no emotional instability whatever we experience has some kind of permanency. Things are not so temporary. In some ways, the less we expect things to be permanent, the more we begin to see them as quite permanent. It's like waiting for a friend. The more quickly we want him or her to turn up, the longer it takes, but if we just relax, it is so quick. It depends upon our own subjective attitude. Obviously, if we don't get disappointed each time something happens, that will lead to happiness or joy and then to the discovery of self, which is discovering who we are. That seems to be the order.

QUESTION: I'm having trouble with why you're calling the identity crisis "selflessness."

RINPOCHE: Our ordinary notion of self is no "self" at all. That is why it is called selflessness. What we normally think we are is not our self. The more we manufacture a notion of self, the less we have a clear idea about who we are. The labels we put on ourselves just turn out to be labels, nothing more. Early Buddhism says everything is selfless, everything is impermanent, everything is suffering. Yogacara is saying, "Yes, that is true on the samsaric level, but if you pulled up your socks you could see the whole thing in quite a different light." What we normally experience as impermanent turns out to be relatively permanent, what we normally experience as suffering turns out to be no suffering at all, and selflessness does not destroy you, you begin to discover your own basic nature and well-being. Yogacara philosophy is making a positive statement.

QUESTION: In your book *The Four Dharmas of Gampopa*, you said a meditator goes through three basic stages. First you see neuroses as a tremendous hassle and something to eradicate, then you gain glimpses of basic sanity through your neurosis, and finally you see that neuroses are the mind itself. Does Yogacara relate to the first two stages and tantra to the third?

RINPOCHE: No, Yogacara deals with the last two in some sense, while tantra deals with the last two in greater detail. This transformation of neurosis into wisdom really goes back to Yogacara philosophy but tantra expounds on it in greater detail.

QUESTION: Could you expand on your comment that Yogacara differed from the more general Buddhist thinking of the time.

RINPOCHE: Early Buddhists saw a sharp distinction between samsara and nirvana. If you are in samsara you need to get out, so to speak. You marvel at nirvana and see its attainment as only a remote possibility at some stage in the future. Nirvana is also described as the cessation of neurosis and suffering. The Madhyamaka School of later Buddhism said that neuroses really do not have any essential nature because they are basically empty. There is no substance to your neuroses so you can work with them from that perspective because the more you understand that your neuroses are substanceless, the more you are able to free yourself from them. There was no talk about the transformation of neuroses into wisdom in the Madhyamaka view. The Yogacarins were the ones who said that neuroses can be transformed into wisdom. Neurosis and wisdom do not have to be viewed as conflictual because the proper management of your neurosis would be to transform it into wisdom.

QUESTION: Don't the tantric schools that are based on Madhyamaka philosophy also talk about transformation?

RINPOCHE: There are differences within the tantric traditions as well. Some tantric traditions hold Madhyamaka to be the ultimate solution while others have a lot more sympathy for Yogacara philosophy. Nonetheless, almost all the tantric traditions are indebted to Yogacara philosophy. In other words, on a practical level, most of the tantras would agree, but on the ultimate level, they might have some disagreement.

QUESTION: Isn't tantra also a practice used by magicians and shamans?

RINPOCHE: The tantras did develop in a climate where there were a lot of magicians but their practices are much more sophisticated than primitive magic. The Buddhist tantras are in keeping with Buddhist philosophy. Hindu tantras are in keeping with Samkhya and yoga philosophies. The Buddhist and Hindu tantras are not arbitrary practices that developed out of primitive practices. They did use some local practices, but that element of it was in fact quite arbitrary in some sense.

QUESTION: Do Yogacarin and Madhyamika viewpoints both lead to enlightenment?

RINPOCHE: All of these approaches lead to enlightenment. It's just a matter of deciding which approach is palatable for you from a practical perspective. People might debate about whether Yogacara or Madhyamaka has the ultimate solution but that is purely theoretical. On the practical side it is quite different.

QUESTION: For practitioners, the Yogacara viewpoint may be easier to relate to because it talks about the self and aspects of mind, whereas Madhyamaka doesn't deal with that sort of thing.

RINPOCHE: That's right. That's why there has been a lot of debate between Yogacarins and Madhyamikas. To talk about the "self" is almost revolutionary but Yogacarins do not mean any kind of metaphysical notion of self. They just mean you have developed a healthy attitude toward yourself and no longer suffer from any kind of identity crisis. Yogacarins say that as soon as we give up the notion of self or stop getting neurotic about ourselves, we begin to become content with who we are and stop striving to be someone else. The more we appreciate who we are, the more we come closer to who we are, which is discovering our own being. If we stop formulating metaphysical notions of the soul or cease to get worked up about ourselves, and begin to appreciate who we are without striving toward achieving something or being someone we are not, we will appreciate our present situation and become more the person we actually are. The ability to appreciate ourselves leads to a healthy attitude toward oneself. The more we try to be someone else, the more destructive it gets.

In history, a lot of famous or artistic people have committed suicide because they were trying to be someone else. You might start thinking, "There are so many Buddhist schools and they all seem opposed to each other," but you have to look at it from an overall perspective. Even from an individual practitioner's point of view, the different Buddhist schools are chronological. We start on the early Buddhist level and learn about impermanence, selflessness, suffering, and so on. We then get onto the mahayana level and learn about Madhyamaka or Yogacara. Then we proceed from there to the tantric level and look at the whole thing from yet another perspective. The development is a gradual one, both from an historical and a personal point of view. We don't get into Buddhist practice arbitrarily; we start from somewhere and then continue to somewhere. Buddhists do not see any contradiction in that because it is an evolutionary process. If we were to just extract certain aspects from different schools we would get really confused because we will not see the overall structure. That seems to be a point we have to keep in mind.

QUESTION: Are you saying that Yogacara and Madhyamaka don't really disagree; it's just a matter of emphasis?

RINPOCHE: Fundamentally, that's right. Theoretically they agree in some sense, but practically they are quite different. The approaches and emphases are quite different. Madhyamikas do not emphasize the mind and practice as much as Yogacarins do. Yogacara always talks about the mind, whereas for Madhyamaka both mind and matter are unreal.

QUESTION: In the Zen tradition, the whole thing is to realize your basic nature, which is emptiness. That seems to correlate with Madhyamaka yet Zen is very practice-orientated.

RINPOCHE: Zen Buddhists seem to have been more influenced by Yogacara than by Madhyamaka. I think that is true historically as well. They were familiar with Madhyamaka philosophy but when they talk about understanding the nature of the mind, they talk about "zen mind" or "no-mind" because the mind you discover is not "mind" from the ordinary point of view. It is not the mind you have understood in the past; it is something different. It is the discovery of your own nature in some sense. They do not say that mind is totally empty as Madhyamikas do. Madhyamikas leave no room for an acknowledgment of the nature of mind. If you want to be a thoroughgoing prasangika you would have to demolish that as well because it would disturb your conceptual paraphernalia.

QUESTION: Does neurosis vanish once we transform it?

RINPOCHE: Neuroses get dispersed as you keep working with them with a healthy attitude. If you have a negative attitude toward your neuroses, that is only another neurotic act that creates further neuroses. You need to have a proper attitude toward your own neurosis, which means you need to have some sympathy toward it. You don't necessarily encourage it, but just acknowledge the presence of the neurosis. You could say, "Neurosis is bad, forget about it," but then it hits you in the face when you least expect it, so you just can't ignore it. The best thing to do is acknowledge its presence and not get too worked up about it. If you get worked up about your neurosis, you will become more neurotic and finally get completely mired in it. A healthy attitude is necessary.

QUESTION: Does that mean the neurosis dissipates through understanding it or seeing it for what it is?

RINPOCHE: That is precisely the distinction between absolute and relative truth actually. We don't even know our own neuroses; we have not really properly discovered them. We think we know everything about our neurosis and don't want to know any more about it, but the fact is we don't know enough about it. We don't really know what the neurosis is; we just know what it appears to be. That is the distinction between absolute and relative truth. We know the appearance, the way it is presented to us, but we don't know what it is really about, what it really is. We discover what neuroses really are through dealing with them with a healthy attitude. We must not look at neurosis from a neurotic viewpoint; we need to view it from a healthy viewpoint.

QUESTION: Would Yogacarins say that what neuroses really are is that which pervades all phenomena?

RINPOCHE: I think it's the other way around actually. Basic awareness or buddhanature is something everyone possesses. It is not personal; it pervades everyone. We are intrinsically all the same and neuroses just happen to be there incidentally. We don't know what neuroses are all about, just that neuroses exist. The reason they are incidental is because the moment we begin to realize what neuroses are, they begin to dissipate. If they were something real, they couldn't dissipate, they would continue to exist. If something is real, it must exist indefinitely. But a neurosis is something that can come to an end and it comes to an end is through proper assessment. Neuroses can be worked with in this way because even they are permeated by our own intrinsic, basic awareness. That gives us the possibility of working with them.

QUESTION: What's the basic difference between Madhyamaka and Yogacara?

RINPOCHE: The real difference is that Yogacarins leave room for the existence of the mind in an ultimate sense whereas Madhyamikas do not. Madhyamikas say, "Just look at the insubstantiality of neuroses; they come and go." It's not because your mother didn't breastfeed you long enough that you have become neurotic. It's not because of past experiences so much as your own preoccupation with that neurosis now, in the present state, either subconsciously or consciously, that is causing all the problems. That is why you happen to be neurotic. Those things come and go. They are unsubstantial. They are empty. You contemplate that. With the Yogacarins, you explore it further because just saying "neuroses are empty" is not good enough. You must see what they are all about. What is that neurotic tendency? Where is it coming from? How is it making you suffer? What is the nature of that neurosis? You try to work with it rather than say it is empty.

QUESTION: Don't Madhyamaka and tantra both involve working on the space that neurosis happens in rather than worrying about the neurosis?

RINPOCHE: The practice side of tantra is very much connected with Yogacara, but philosophically, most of tantra would go along with Madhyamaka because it would agree that even the mind is empty in the ultimate sense.

QUESTION: Is a healthy attitude the same as what Chogyam Trungpa Rinpoche calls "sacred outlook"?

RINPOCHE: That is tantric language. That sort of thing comes along on the tantric level. But yes, it is the germinal aspect of it, in some sense. You have a basic healthy attitude toward the neurosis. You might not regard it as sacred because that is much more than relating to it in a friendly manner. Sacred outlook is almost to respect our neurosis, which is hard to do.

That approach comes at later stage because it is a much more daring approach. But Yogacara sowed the seed for that notion before tantra developed.

For Madhyamaka, there is no "being" to be discovered; we have just manufactured this whole notion of self and it does not exist at all. There is not even any ground upon which we could build up a notion of self. Yogacarins say we deviated from our basic being. We thought we needed some kind of self and strived toward it but it turned out to be fiction. We discover what we are by just being who we are. Normally we try to discover ourselves through painting or playing music or writing. Yogacarins say that type of notion is totally mistaken. We don't discover who we are that way. We do so simply through appreciating our present situation, appreciating our own basic being, without trying to be someone other than who we are.

QUESTION: You said we keep trying to find out who we are through some sort of activity. What makes this process not frustrating?

RINPOCHE: When you work with neuroses, your motivation is not to have this gigantic self as a project you want to complete, it's just a way of relating to your present situation, to being what you are. You look into yourself and explore your neuroses instead of saying, "These neuroses should not be there." You should not regard them as aliens who happened to invade your basic being. You should regard them as part of yourself. As you become more hospitable toward your own sneuroses, you will begin to become gentle and sympathetic toward yourself as well. You will begin to accept yourself much more, and the more you accept yourself, the more you will come into close contact with who you are. It is not a linear process, you are going inward, looking closely at who you are. Even spiritual practices are normally used to go from *A* to *B*, but in this case, you go inward.

QUESTION: When you are doing this process of working inward are you seeking some sort of ideal state?

RINPOCHE: The difference between this kind of notion of self and our ordinary notion of self is that our ordinary notion of self is divisive. Everything is put into pigeonholes: "this is my emotional instability," "this is my neurosis," "this is my body," "this is my mind," "this is my brain," "this is my head." Then you discover there is no "you" at all. But in this case you become much more encompassing. Whatever you experience, that is you. You can't say, "This is my neurosis." The neurosis is not something apart from you so you cannot make that division. That is much more expansive and hospitable, which is a healthy sign.

This leads to the tantric notion of "divine pride." When you visualize deities, you take pride in yourself as being the deity. This type of pride is not ordinary pride, where you think you are better than some else, it is just a basic sense of well-being. Yogacarins sowed the seed for this kind of notion. You feel good about yourself, you don't feel negative, which is totally destructive anyway. If you have an ordinary notion of self or pride, you become critical. You might become so critical about your practice that it ceases to make any headway. You practice so much but you are critical—you could do better—so you begin to punish yourself, which is totally nondharmic or non-Buddhist. If you feel good about your practice, feel good about yourself, and feel good about your surroundings, this is the discovery of that other type of self. With the ordinary self, we always reject or discriminate or make judgments or punish ourselves. Normally we punish ourselves all the time through that notion of self. It is always criticizing us. "You are not doing this, you are not doing that, you are bad." The fact is we criticize ourselves much more than anyone else would criticize us.

QUESTION: Doesn't the word *tantra* literally mean "thread" or "continuity"?

RINPOCHE: Yes, because in some ways, even the attainment of enlightenment isn't a dead end. Tantra really means "enlightenment is a continual process;" it is a dynamic process rather than a matter of coming to a dead end and saying, "This is it."

Four Factors of Basic Being

The four factor of basic being are said to be purity (*tsang*), joy (*de*), permanence (*tag*), and ego (*dag*), and it might help to go into some detail about these things before we proceed any further. We can try to gain some understanding of what it really means when it is said, "Impurity is transformed into purity, misery into joy," and so on.

PURITY

When Yogacarins talk about purity, they are not looking at it from some moralistic point of view. This concept refers much more to a psychological purity than to a moral dictum as such. It means we are able to understand the nature of ourselves and look inward rather than just looking outward and labeling things arbitrarily. If we can see the positive side of a situation instead of seeing evil in others, this will obviously transform our perception of the world. Instead of looking at everything in an impure way, our perception is transformed into pure perception.

It said that the more we perceive negativities in situations and other people, the more frustrated we will become. There is that kind of correlation between what takes place inside us and what takes place outside us. What takes place inside us depends upon what is taking place outside us and how we view those things. We cannot really know what other people are like since we can only see how someone behaves or what someone does. Just using someone's external behavior as a criterion for judging what they are really like is mistaken. Instead of doing that, we should look inside ourselves and try to work out how we assess different situations. It is said that the more we appreciate situations and other people, the less egocentric we become. When we are unable to do this, we become more egocentric and demanding. To overcome one is to overcome the other. When it is said, "You should appreciate the situation," that doesn't mean we have to look it at as good or bad or something of that sort. We should just look at the situation as it is rather than expecting it to be something other than what it is.

JOY

Pure perception leads to the notion of joy, which is not understood as a euphoric kind of state. Normally we think joy is something that needs to be sought or acquired at some stage in the future, but in this sense joy is discovered within ourselves rather than externally. We tend to think that if certain situations came about we will be joyous or happy. If we had a holiday house next to the sea, we would be happy, or if we were to get a job promotion, we would be happy. Sometimes when we become spiritually inclined that attitude gets translated into spiritual terms, so that instead of talking about holiday houses we talk about nirvana, and instead of talking about job promotion we think about the bhumis.

Attitudes such as that are regarded as a non-joyous approach. The situation that is already present is not being assessed so joy is unable to manifest. Joy comes about only when we are able to accept a situation as it is, which is not a matter of giving up hope or giving into in despair, but a question of relating to the present situation properly instead of hoping that if a situation was something other than it is, it would be much more joyous than what we are experiencing now. It is said that if we seek joy or happiness we are not going to obtain it. In the scriptures, it says we have been seeking happiness ever since we were born, but we have not obtained it because we are searching for it, instead of giving ourselves a break by just looking at the current situation and discovering it. A lot of people die as seekers of happiness without ever attaining it.

PERMANENCE

That leads to "permanence," which is called *tag pa* or *tag*. Permanence might create the image of eternalism. It might give the impression that we are going to be joyous forever, that if we fulfill certain conditions we will be "blissed-out" for the rest of our lives. But here permanence really means being in the moment and not brooding about past situations or chasing after the future. As they say, "tomorrow never comes." When tomorrow comes it is already today so tomorrow is never present. The past does not exist either because it is no longer there. Normally we are unable to be in the present; we either brood over past situations or chase after the future. Past experiences leave traces and dispositions that influence our present situation because we are unable to accept that situation as it come along.

The past influences us because we were unable to make a proper assessment of a situation when it arose. Since the situation did not get resolved we are still haunted by it in the present. For instance, if we went on a cruise and had a nice trip, we would feel happy about it and it would not influence our present situation. However, if we had a bad childhood due to an aggressive father, this might color our vision and the way we view other people. Even if a situation like that has not been resolved, the way a particular person behaves, the way he smokes or drinks tea, might still trigger memories of our father. It is said we will carry present experiences into the future in an unhealthy way if we do not make a proper assessment of the present. We can only make a proper assessment of a situation when we are able to live in the present and not dwell in the past or future.

There is a story in one of the Buddhist sutras about a man being chased by a tiger. He runs away, jumps off a cliff, and discovers he is able to hang onto a strawberry plant. He looks down and sees a deep abyss, and then he looks up and sees the tiger looking down at him from at the edge of the cliff. Suddenly a rat starts eating at the root of the strawberry plant. The man looks up, and then he looks down, and then he pops one of the strawberries in his mouth and says, "How wonderful." Buddha says that the past and the future are like the deep abyss below and the tiger above and we just have to live in the present like that man and enjoy the strawberry. As soon as he falls, he is not going to be there to suffer, what has happened is already in the past and the tiger will fail to get him.

HEALTHY EGO

Those situations lead to the discovery of healthy ego. The healthy ego is encompassing rather than fragmented like our normal conscious experiences. It is also much more centered and encompasses both the unconscious and conscious side of ourselves. Normally when people talk about superego or self, they are referring to where consciousness resides or to whom consciousness belongs. In this case, no distinction is made between the two. Consciousness is the healthy ego and the healthy ego is consciousness. It is not only consciousness but the unconscious side as well. The substratum of awareness is not a fully conscious experience as such, but all those things are covered by the notion of the healthy ego.

The more the practitioner looks into the whole situation, the more he or she will discover the field of consciousness. You will be able to realize that your normal ego is just a small fraction of the entire structure of consciousness. It is said that egocentric mentation, which normally creates all these egocentric tendencies, gets transformed into the "wisdom of equanimity," which is to be understood as having a healthy ego at this particular point. Later on we can discuss the meaning of the wisdom of equanimity in more detail. We can also see here that Yogacara philosophy had an influence on Buddhist tantra because the notions of the five wisdoms—mirrorlike wisdom, the wisdom of equanimity, discriminating wisdom, all-accomplishing wisdom, and wisdom of dharmadhatu—are an essential part of tantric psychology. The Yogacarins were the first to formulate these ideas.

QUESTIONS

QUESTION: What do you mean by "tantric psychology"?

RINPOCHE: Tantric ideas are about how the mind functions and how certain visualizations enable you to tap into certain psychological resources. Normally these are divided into five categories of wisdom. Most of the time these practices are directed to the discovery how our ordinary way of relating to things can be transformed by changing our consciousness.

QUESTION: Does living in the present mean that you don't plan for the future?

RINPOCHE: You still need to plan for the future but the point is that a lot of people do not live in the present at all. That is why it is said, "The present is permanent." Normally we do not have any experience of permanence. We might go after permanence, but in fact, we are not living at all. We don't experience what we are supposed to experience because we are not living in the present, which means we are unable to live at all. We are either dwelling in the past or projecting ourselves into the future. Living in the present doesn't necessarily mean the future is forgotten. In some ways, if we live in the present properly, the future is already in the present. What we do in the present is much more important because that is what will influence our future. We could have some vision about what we will do in the future but it is what we do now that will make the difference.

QUESTION: When you plan for the future, you don't dwell on it day and night, but a moment comes when you say, "What am I going to do tomorrow?" Are those thoughts dwelling in the future or in the present?

RINPOCHE: No one is saying we shouldn't think about the future at all, they are saying we normally do not even realize that we are living in the past or the future. In some ways, the moment you realize you do those things you already have one foot in the present. A lot of people are too speedy even to realize where they are projecting their thoughts. We get so worked up and neurotic that we speed round and around until we lose perspective on the whole situation and then we can't make a proper assessment of the future either. We are moving faster than we can keep up with ourselves.

QUESTION: Is joy a meditative state of mind or can it be a normal everyday situation?

RINPOCHE: Joy is related to the meditative state of mind—to shamatha experience—but it is not particularly euphoric; it's just a general sense of well-being. That is much more satisfying than being elated one minute and depressed the next, which is a kind of psychotic tendency. Manic depressives experience that sort of thing. Our normal experiences tend to be a bit like that too. Joy is just a general sense of well-being, being able to accept the situation that is presented to us, without wishing it was something different. We sometimes become quite petty. If a person is laughing we say, "Why are you laughing when I'm miserable?" If a person is crying we say, "Why are you crying when that just puts a greater burden on the existing suffering?" If your house is facing north, you want it to face south. We need to learn just to relate to the existing situation and feel really good about it. That applies to yourself as well. If you feel really good, you don't wish you were doing something else or that you were more intelligent or this and that. In a way being yourself is the most natural thing to do, but I don't think we can accept that, in some sense.

QUESTION: Sometimes you suggest joy has a reference point, when things such as meditation inspire you, then other times you say joy doesn't have a reference point and is self-manifesting.

RINPOCHE: Well, at the beginning there has to be some kind of reference point, but it becomes more and more part of yourself. The initial excitement might wear out, but your experience of that feeling might get extended as it becomes more and more stable. That's the whole point. For example, to do prostrations does not actually produce joy, but in some ways it excites joy or brings it to the fore, or you begin to discover it. The prostration is not producing it. If you take drugs, the feeling is produced by that particular agency, but prostrations are not like that. They are the means you use to discover your own innate qualities. All those practices are related with that type of situation because you can't produce something that is not there.

QUESTION: Often our suffering is stimulated by another person, where we get caught up in resentment or anger. How do you deal with that situation in a Buddhist way?

RINPOCHE: Most of the time some kind of habitual process is set up and it becomes very difficult to work with that effectively. A person does something and you react in a particular way. The best thing is to work on more minor situations and in time try to apply it to that person. In the meanwhile, all you can do is try to be aware. Before you react, try to be aware of how you are reacting and if you are still reacting in the usual way. Try to be aware before you react or even while you are reacting. If you discover you are doing the same thing as usual, you could stop that situation. But in the long run, I think it's a matter of getting out of the habitual process. All the alternatives prove to be equally unsatisfactory. If you react each time the other person does something or the other person reacts each time you do something, the situation gets worse and worse. Your reactions to that person are not solving the situation. In fact, it makes the situation worse and worse until it becomes unbearable. It's really common sense logic. Why do it? If the other person does keep reacting habitually that does not mean you have to follow suit. Just say, "This is not solving anything." You might feel you are giving in and the situation is hopeless or you are accepting the situation through hopelessness, but I think if you can do that, you will feel much better in time. There is a difference between giving up and accepting the situation. Giving up is about lack of confidence or helplessness. Once you begin to accept the whole situation, you might gradually develop a different way of looking at it. You can't expect miracles on the spot but things do change that way. A lot of the time, we act in the same way, but if we adopt a new way of looking at the whole thing, if we adopt a new stance, we are able to see the same situation in a different light. It happens constantly in our ordinary experience.

QUESTION: Could you say something about applying these things because sometimes practice seems to just heighten one's neurotic tendencies.

RINPOCHE: Sometimes, when we try to apply these things, we might think we are making no progress or that in some ways we are becoming more neurotic in terms of dealing with certain situations, but those things are really part of the process itself. In some sense, you are becoming more aware. You have to be gentle with yourself, instead of feeling how bad the whole situation is and that the interaction between yourself and others is unhealthy. Instead of feeling claustrophobic with that whole situation, you need to let in a bit of fresh air, treat that sensitivity with gentleness, and accept it. We have to relate to situations; otherwise we are going to feel more and more bogged down. However, if you are able to really relate to it and accept it, it becomes a different situation.

QUESTION: But that requires the utmost skill. When I go out of this room and repeat that idea to myself, this little voice will pop up in the back of my mind and say, "Who are you trying to kid?"

RINPOCHE: Sometimes it is good to be critical of your practice and your progress because you might be deluded into thinking you are doing something fantastic. At the same time, our tendency is to become really self-critical. We become more and more critical and then we are unable to relate to the whole situation properly. Sometimes those things crop up because we are too concerned about the other person. I think martyrdom manifests in a crude form. Sometimes we have to accept the situation and not feel that we are responsible for everything, because we could go the other way and think everything is created by us, that we are the worst person or we are not making a proper assessment of the situation. That is another egocentric approach. Because we wish that we were different, because we wish that we had more capabilities to deal with the situation, we are expecting the situation to be something other than it is. The best thing to do is say, "This is how it is but there is no need for me to feel responsible and carry the whole burden."

QUESTION: Working through things in oneself doesn't always lead to the environment being dynamic because the other party may have very fixed ideas and not even recognize the possibility of movement.

RINPOCHE: You could do certain things to try to help the other person but a lot of the time it doesn't work. Instead of having two stubborn people, it's best if there is only one. Sometimes people can't be changed, so instead of keeping on at it, the best thing to do is have a healthy attitude and not expect any dramatic change. That happens a lot. That's why changing your own way of looking at things can make all those situations less serious. As they say, "It takes two to tango." If the other person is left to shadow box the air, he or she might realize something from that also.

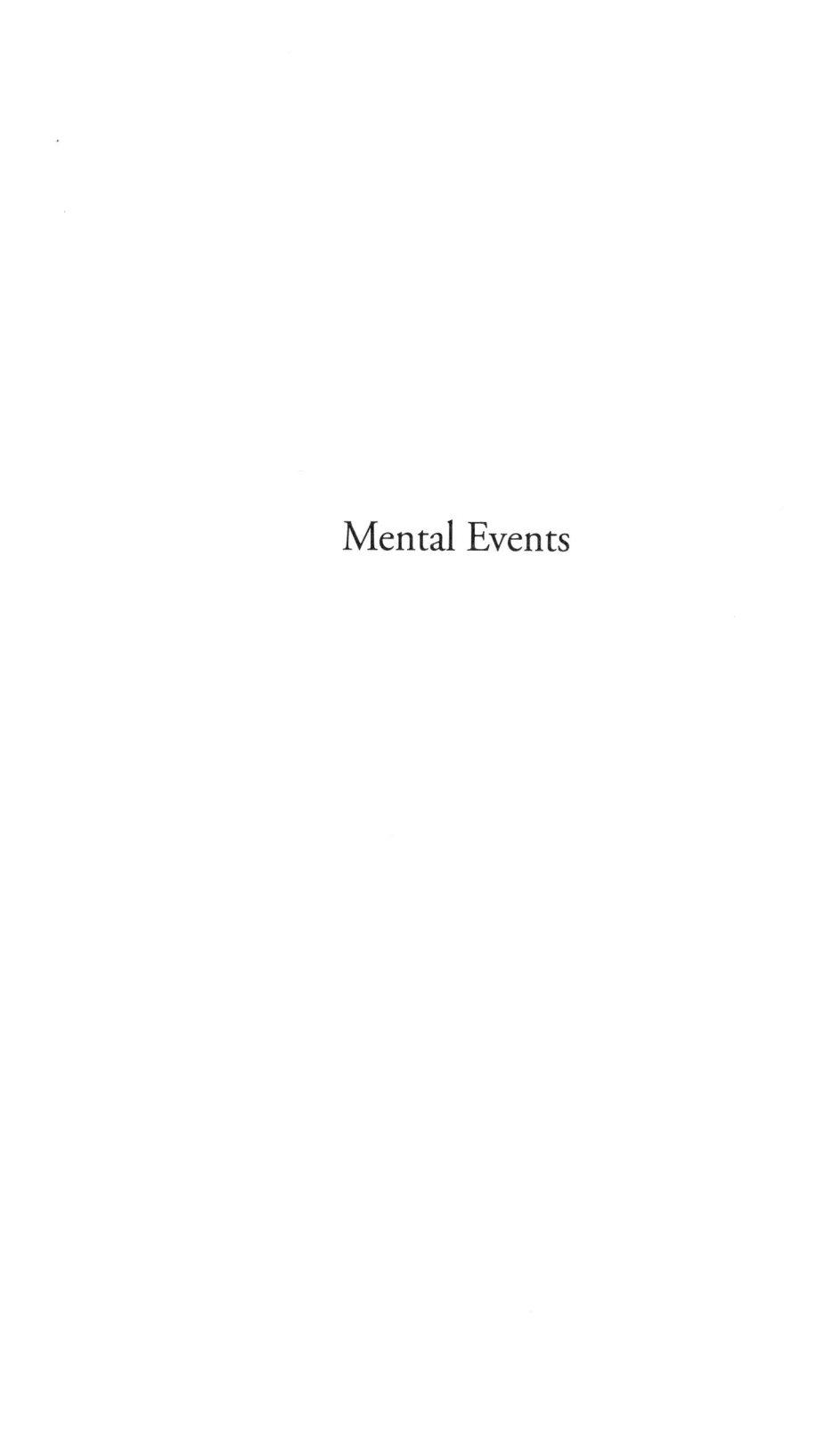

Mental Events

Five Omnipresent Mental Events

Having concluded our discussion on the mind we can venture into a discussion on the mental events. It may be appropriate to mention that when Buddhists talk about mental events, they base the discussions on their own experiences, upon an introspective method. In the West this type of approach has been questioned. Academic psychologists particularly feel that the introspective method is completely invalid because you cannot observe what a person is feeling and you cannot actually display what you are feeling to others. Introspective methods are also deemed untrustworthy because one person might experience something in one way and another person might experience that same thing as something else, which makes it very difficult to come to any consensus.

The Buddhist approach seems to be quite different. We don't talk about mental processes from the perspective of how everyone else experiences them; we discuss the experiences of individuals in the context of meditating and working through our own preconceptions and so on. Whatever is said in Buddhist texts is not prejudiced; they are the statements of unbiased individuals. The introspective method needs to be re-evaluated in some sense, because despite the popularity of Freud and Jung, it is regarded as extremely questionable by many academic psychologists. As we can see in these discussions, Buddhists adopted a form of this introspective method.

As a result of examining consciousness through methods of introspection, Yogacarins isolated five mental events that accompany all of our perceptions. As they accompany any type of perceptual experience, they are described as the five omnipresents (*kun cho nga*). Two of the five omnipresents—feeling-tone and conception—were discussed in the chapter on the five skandhas.

FEELING-TONE

To reiterate what was said in chapter four, all our experience have some kind of feeling-tone—whether it is pleasurable, nonpleasurable, or neutral—and Buddhists make distinction between the mental and physical aspects of these three types of feeling. This is interesting because in the West people have tried to reduce bodily feelings to mind and mental feelings to organic things. A perfect example of this can be seen in the way psychoanalysis attempt to ascribe all types of tension, anxiety, suffering, and pain to a psychological model. They never refer to our physical aspect. Behaviorists, on the other hand, try to reduce all mental processes to the physical level.

As far as Buddhists are concerned it does not have to be explained that way. We have bodily pain and bodily pleasure as well as mental pain and mental pleasure and those two things are correlated. For common sense people that are not professional psychologists or philosophers this might sound simple enough because that is how we actually experience things; it is really quite straightforward.

You might be surprised though if you read the standard Western texts on this topic. The whole topic has become a hotbed of debate, where people try to work out whether our painful experiences are a bodily situation or a mental situation. It is really quite an interesting thing to contemplate. A lot of books try to explain all of our mental processes through physiological descriptions. When you get angry, certain glands operate and squirt hormones, and so on. Other texts try to explain everything through our unconscious activities, where whatever you experience has something to do with your unconscious drive and things like that.

In any case, the Buddhist approach acknowledges two types of feeling—physical and mental—and says they are correlated. Another interesting thing that Buddhists say is that a feeling-tone does not come about accidentally, but arises as a result of a particular cause. There is a reason why we experience pain and there is a reason why we experience pleasure. These things don't take place accidentally so we cannot complain about them. Normally if we experience pain, we complain that someone else is responsible or some situation is responsible. But there are reasons for that pain that relate to our own personal history, that relate to things we have done in the past, and to the things that we are doing now—things that have caused certain situations to take place that result in either pain or pleasure, be it mental or physical.

CONCEPTION

The next omnipresent mental factor is conception. As we discussed, conception is related to the discursive faculty of mind; the mind that tries to categorize things, to put everything into pigeonholes and have a neat world. Everything is a package deal, everything is neat and tidy; there are no loose ends. In some individuals this is very much the case; everything is buckled down and compartmentalized so that there is no room for movement or flexibility. That is conception, which is also an aspect of the five skandhas.

DIRECTIONALITY OF MIND

We now move onto the mental factors that are particularly important aspects of the five omnipresents. The first is known as the directionality of mind (*sem pa*). Buddhists say mind is active and creative rather than passive and receptive. This is what directionality of mind means. If you are walking down the street and notice something in a showcase you might think the object is impinging on your visual sense organ, but Yogacara psychology says mind is by nature creative. You direct your mind to a particular object rather than having your attention drawn by the object. We say, "My attention was drawn to this object, I couldn't draw my mind." However, your psychological processes directed your mind to that object. That is directionality of mind and it includes psychological processes as well as objects. Whether they are healthy or unhealthy, we direct our attention to those mental events as well. Mind by nature is constitutive or creative.

EGOCENTRIC DEMANDING

The fourth mental factor is known as egocentric demanding (*yi la je pa*). Directionality of mind is related to the perception of an object as a whole while egocentric demanding is directed at the specific characteristics of that object. Normally we might think that a particular object interests us, "This is what I want." If it is a piece of chocolate, we think, "I would like chocolate." We might go for it but we do not go for the chocolate as a whole. There is some characteristic such as nuts or a certain taste that draws our interest. We do not just go for the chocolate by itself. We might direct our mind to the chocolate and think, "That is chocolate," but there is a particular reason why we take an interest in it such as how it looks or how it tastes. Two situations are therefore involved. The difference between directionality of mind and egocentric demanding is the transition from the general to the specific.

RAPPORT

The last mental factor is known as rapport. *Rapport* means "a sense organ, an object, and a consciousness becomes unified within our experience." Whenever we experience something,

Five Omnipresent Mental Events

there is an object, an appropriate sense organ, and the consciousness that accompanies those two factors. These three things therefore converge at the point of rapport. It is said that rapport is not a totally discursive or intellectual process; it provides the possibility for feeling to arise. So there is a feeling-tone as well as a cognitive aspect involved.

Traditional Western psychologists used to distinguish between cognitive and affective mental faculties—*affective* meaning the "emotional aspect" and *cognitive* meaning the "discursive or intellectual aspect"—but as far as Buddhists are concerned, we cannot make a distinction between these two. For instance, behavioral psychologists have conducted experiments putting rats through a T-shaped maze. On one end of the *T* they placed food and on the other end of the *T* they placed a gadget that gave the rat an electric shock. The experimenters sent the rats through the body of the maze, and at first the rats would go either way, either to the food or to the electric shock, but after a while they invariably went only to the food. The psychologists concluded that rats have some cognitive ability but they excluded the affective side completely. How did the rat feels? That was totally excluded. As long as the rat went the right way, they thought, "This rat has intelligence." But even we can observe that rats are terrified.

However a lot of people, to this day, make sharp distinctions between cognitive and affective states of mind. Buddhists do not make this distinction. They say that if the mind executes some cognitive act; an affective aspect must accompany it. If you withdraw from a particular stimulus, such as an electric shock, you withdraw not just because of your body or nervous system; you also withdraw because of how you feel when that stimulus is experienced. It is as simple as that. So in this case, in terms of rapport, consciousness has the aspect of being both cognitive and affective.

These mental factors are called "five omnipresents" because they accompany all of our mental activities. Without them we cannot experience anything. First we direct our mind to a particular object, then we direct it to a certain characteristic of that object, and then a rapport has to take place. There is a feeling-tone involved as well as a conceptual process that classifies the whole situation. The five omnipresents accompany every mental activity.

QUESTIONS

QUESTION: Why does mind fixate on one object as opposed to another?

RINPOCHE: Because of the directionality of mind; we direct our mind to a particular object because of that mental factor. It's a common saying, "My attention was drawn to this object." But why not to some other object? If objects simply impinged on your visual organ, you would direct your mind arbitrarily to any object, but that does not happen. You direct your mind to a particular object. That has a lot to do with your traces and dispositions.

You drag your mind to a particular object deliberately. Most of the time, we drag our mind to an object we have dragged our mind to all along. People who like clothes always stop by a clothing shop. They might just be walking along and suddenly they pass a clothing shop and they turn and look. When I pass along the street, I look at the bookshops. First, you just notice the clothing shop, then you drag your mind toward it, but then certain clothing might interest you. You just don't go in and buy arbitrarily; certain things will interest you. When you drag your mind toward a particular object, this is egocentric demanding. If I go into a bookshop, I don't just buy any book. Egocentric demanding would be demanding "something." If you are vegetarian, you always notice vegetarian food stores, but not other restaurants. If you are interested in Chinese food, you notice the Chinese restaurants. It's as simple as that.

It is said that "the mind is constitutive," because we drag our mind toward a particular object. There has been a lot of debate about whether the mind is passive or active. Buddhists would say mind is active. There are others who say mind is like a mirror that reflects all images but doesn't direct itself at all; it is just passive and receptive. Information just comes from the object and feeds into the cerebral and mental faculties. Buddhists say the mind is constitutive because it has the capacity to be selective. That's what it all it boils down to: mind has the capacity to be selective. You just don't go around making arbitrary choices, you selectively make certain choices.

QUESTION: Are you saying that if you are in a situation where a large amount of information is available to you, the things you fix your mind on in are your decision?

RINPOCHE: At a football match, all these people are there, but different people drag their minds toward different things. These people are there by some general consensus, they all like to watch football, but you will discover that some people go there to watch the crowd, others to watch the football players, and others to watch other things. They all drag their attention toward certain things. There might be something that makes them drag their attention toward it but then egocentric demand makes that attention more specific. There are feeling-tones involved as well. If the players on the opposition side kick the football in the right way, you might react violently. There are feeling-tones on that level. The crowd in general might create a certain feeling-tone or mood. You can't experience anything without some kind of feeling-tone. All the other mental factors are involved as well. You categorize and pigeonhole things, because unless you do so, you will not be able to make distinctions between one thing and another.

Everything is compartmentalized in some way. We all do that, but some people do it more than others. Everyone has all the mental factors, but some people have certain mental factors as a predominant characteristic. If you are intellectual by nature, conception might be a predominant characteristic.

If you are an emotional person, feeling-tone might be your predominant characteristic. When we say that someone is an observant person, what do we mean by observant? Maybe directionality of mind and egocentric demands are predominant in those people. But that doesn't mean that someone who is observant does not feel anything. Just because you are so neat and tidy and have everything categorized does not mean you don't have other characteristics. There are degrees of those mental factors.

The traces and dispositions determine which factor will predominate. All the mental factors are influenced by your past experiences. They have left traces and dispositions, so you feel in a certain way and your feeling cannot be shared by others, because they are your feelings. That is the result of your own traces and dispositions. Someone else feels another way because of their traces and dispositions. You conceptualize in a particular way and that is your way. Someone else does the opposite and that is his or her way of conceptualizing. This type of thing is always happening.

However, as we said, the mental factors are subsidiary; the mind is more important. When we talk about mental events, we always have to keep the eight levels of consciousness in view. They play the most important role because all the other mental factors are influenced by them. When we discuss healthy and unhealthy mental factors, it depends upon how the mental factors are managed. Certain mental factors would leave healthy and wholesome traces and dispositions and other mental factors would leave unwholesome and unhealthy traces and dispositions. That is how our life is influenced.

QUESTION: I find it a bit depressing when I think that directing my mind to certain objects or having certain feeling responses is predetermined by my traces and dispositions. I feel a like a prisoner of my traces and dispositions.

RINPOCHE: Yogacara philosophy shares this with Freudian

psychoanalysis. With psychoanalysis, you are subject to your drives, instincts, and unconscious tendencies, which create all kinds of anxieties. Yogacara psychology would go along with that to a certain degree. But Freud said you can never dispense with your ordinary suffering; you are stuck with your ordinary experience of traces and dispositions and there is nothing you can do about it. it is only when things get out of control that psychoanalysis can do something. In other words, if you become crazy, psychoanalysis can do something. But everyone is subjected to their instincts and drives and they suffer because of it. Freud said psychoanalysis was not a cure for normal suffering, only for abnormal suffering. The Buddhist approach is that you can cure normal suffering. You can make a proper assessment of your traces and dispositions and see how you are creating them. In some ways, the whole thing is predetermined, but you can also see the way that you are actually imprisoning yourself.

You are also told the best way to approach the whole thing. It is not as if you just observe it and try to work out the best way. Buddhists explain how you can actually work through it, how to see that whole chain reaction happening, and how to make a proper assessment of it. When Buddhists say you are directing your mind to a particular object, they mean that you can also drag your mind to a healthy mental event or an unhealthy mental event. Either way, you leave traces and dispositions, which can be harmful or helpful.

You are able to make that assessment by developing prajna. *Prajna* means "intelligence" rather than intellect, because it is not intellectual activity as such. It is an intelligent way of acting. In some ways, it is related with speculation, I suppose, but it has more to do with action, with how to behave properly. You could be a psychiatrist, but suffer from all kinds of things. You could be a child psychologist, but not understand children at all. Prajna is related to that mental faculty that acts, that is able to make a proper assessment without being too emotionally wrought and without getting carried away intellectually. There is that meeting point, in some sense. That is the faculty you develop, the faculty of being able to make a proper assessment of your mental events.

QUESTION: But isn't that very process of assessing a situation correctly also determined by traces and dispositions?

RINPOCHE: At the beginning it would be, but the more you realize that your activities cannot be predetermined by your traces and dispositions, the more you become free of them. In other words, you can make use of traces and dispositions in a positive way. You do not have to adopt another approach. You make use of your traces and dispositions in a way that is helpful to you rather than misusing them, which is what we normally do. That's the whole point. Normally, we don't even know those things are taking place.

QUESTION: Do you mean we use the traces and dispositions themselves to learn about them so that we can free ourselves from them?

RINPOCHE: Yes, and we direct our mind toward developing feeling-tones that are good for us, such as compassion and love. Those feeling-tones have to be developed. If we have feeling-tones that are emotionally self-defeating, we don't need to develop them. That is how you make use of mental events as well as of traces and dispositions. The more you are able to make a proper assessment of your mental events, the more positive traces and dispositions you will leave on your substratum. Then you will be able to act better. You will be able to act more precisely and accurately. In some ways, this really comes down to saying, "To be able to act means to be able to act intelligently, and to be intelligent means to be able to act properly." Traces and dispositions and all these other things are really being discussed so that we can see how to do these things. As I said, all these things can really be observed. All we have to do is look in and see how they are happening. It's not as if they are inaccessible and we have to do something else to access them. We experience these things all the time so we just look at them to see how they are interrelated and what they are all about.

QUESTION: You said we have feeling-tones that are pleasurable, painful, or indifferent. In a previous lecture, you said that according to the Yogacara School there was no such thing as an indifferent feeling. It was either pleasurable or painful.

RINPOCHE: That is true and it still applies here. Even when we think we are experiencing an indifferent feeling, it is still a feeling. That is what the Yogacarins mean. It does not mean you think you are feeling nothing. People say, "I'm so exhausted from my emotions. I have come to a point where I feel nothing." But how can you feel nothing? That's what you have to look into. When you think you are feeling nothing, as soon as you look into it, how can you feel nothing? It has to be something, either pleasurable or nonpleasurable. It is almost invariably a not pleasurable feeling. That's what the whole thing is all about. Sometimes you consciously feel pleasure, sometimes you consciously feel painful things, and sometimes you feel you don't feel anything. But there is no state where you do not feel anything. Even not feeling anything is a kind of feeling. Otherwise you wouldn't say it.

QUESTION: Some people or some cultures seem to be more emotional than others. How does that relate to this idea of feeling?

RINPOCHE: Again it is because of traces and dispositions. Some cultures are taught to be like that so they become like that. If you look at mathematicians or logicians, their conceptual mental events dominate all their other mental events. But if you look at people who go to primal therapy, they would have more feeling-tones. They want to experience "primal pain" as it is called. There is the primal pain that you experienced as a child but have not experienced since. They say you have to experience primal pain so a great emphasis is placed on feeling-tone on that level. If you talk to these people, they just want to feel; they don't want to do anything else. Sometimes, for those people, feeling and experience become synonymous. To experience means to feel and to feel means to experience.

QUESTION: Would you say that Western cultures are more into the feeling-tone aspect?

RINPOCHE: No, Eastern traditions, whether Hindu or Buddhist, are mostly integrative. They do not make too much distinction between feeling-tones and cognitive faculties. But in the West there is always some kind of dualist approach involved. That is totally anathema to any type of Eastern approach. In the West, so much emphasis is either placed on the body where you become materialistic or the importance is placed on the mind where you become a mentalist. Everything is reduced to mind. Even in the sciences, we have pure mathematics—which you just speculate about and marvel at—and we have applied mathematics. We have pure physics and applied physics. The whole of Western culture, in some way, has that dual approach. Westerners have achieved the optimum level of intellectual exercise. Compared to the East, Westerners really have achieved all kinds of intellectual excellence. But, on the other hand, due to that people experience all kinds of emotional things and become totally emotionally orientated. Buddhists say this has to be integrated. You can't be one way or the other, there has to be some meeting point between the two. You don't become so intellectually orientated that you become a sterile philosopher, as it has been said, and you don't become so emotionally involved that you are blinded by the whole thing.

QUESTION: Do western cultures specialize in generating this egocentric demanding?

RINPOCHE: I think that's a general tendency. I don't think everything the East does is particularly fantastic. It has its own shortcomings. People that take an interest in Eastern cultures and who try to introduce Eastern things into the West should learn that. Again there has to be some kind of meeting point. You can't turn everything into Eastern things or just stick to purely Western things. There has to be some kind of meeting point. People are not able to get what they want out of Western culture without turning to the East, but in the East people are faced with a lot of problems because of their own lack of things.

QUESTION: Conception, apart from categorizing, has the same function as directionality of mind, in terms of directing your mind to a particular object?

RINPOCHE: Most of the time directionality of mind would precede conception. First, your mind gets directed toward a particular object. Then you begin to categorize, label, and draw all kinds of conclusions out of that. Directionality of mind doesn't make distinctions; it isn't discriminatory. Conception is discriminatory. With directionality of mind, your attention is directed toward a particular object. Then conception follows on from that.

QUESTION: From the point of view of Theravada, Buddhism is based on two main structures: the first is *maitri* and the second is this awareness, which ultimately ends in prajna. Is this where you begin to develop awareness?

RINPOCHE: We haven't discussed awareness yet. We haven't said what kind of mental faculty makes you able to assess the whole thing, because it is said people do not have access to that type of mental faculty in ordinary terms. You have to make some effort to acquire that mental faculty. But if you make the effort, you can acquire it. There are only two types of mental events that people don't have access to in normal circumstances. The first one is concentration. We find it so difficult to concentrate on anything. The other one is intelligence or prajna. These two mental factors are something people have to make some kind of effort to develop. All of the others are there. All you have to do is turn your attention inside and really look for them. For example, you don't have to judge all your mental processes in meditation saying, "I'm feeling anger in meditation, so that's bad" and feeling terrible about it or, "I'm thinking about the Buddha, I'm so fantastic."

You need to have an unbiased approach to your meditation. The more you develop that, the more you are able to become objective about your own mental processes. The introspective method itself will then become totally unbiased. You will be able to observe whatever is happening inside you without having to categorize it, without using too much of the mental event of conception. You just observe the whole process. That's why the introspective method becomes valid. Otherwise, as some Western psychologists have said, you could feel one thing and someone else could feel another thing and what would the criterion be for evaluating that? How do you judge the whole thing? A lot of people feel like that too. But if you just constantly observe whatever you experience with an open attitude, you will see that it just comes and goes, and you will be able to make better judgments about how you feel.

QUESTION: Do you analyze anything that arises or just observe it and let it pass?

RINPOCHE: There are two types of meditation. The first is called sitting meditation or shamatha, where you just observe what is going on and see that everything comes and goes. The other one is known as *vipashyana* or "analytical meditation," where you analyze what you experience and question it. You do not necessarily have to sit in meditation posture. You could just be sitting quietly in a corner and questioning whatever you experience; you analyze the feelings that arise. Sitting and analyzing have to go together because sitting meditation makes it possible not jump to conclusions. If you just adopt the analytical approach, you might jump to all kinds of conclusions in a hasty way. But with sitting meditation, you just observe and experience, and analytical meditation enables you to see how the experiences arise and the reasons why they arise. You can see whether the substratum of awareness has anything to do with the whole thing and whether there are such things as traces and dispositions. You have to really question all those things, and if they are there, you have to look into the way they are interrelated. How do the substratum of awareness and the traces and dispositions influence your life?

QUESTION: Can you pick up a day's event and use that as a vipashyana meditation?

RINPOCHE: You can take up any event and see why it has happened. You have to question, "Why has this happened?" You don't stop questioning for any obvious reason. There's always an obvious answer, but you have to question again and again why it happened. "Why is that reason there?" This is the difference between our being intellectual and being intelligent. When you are exercising this sort of thing it is personal. You are trying to learn something for yourself; to learn what the whole thing is all about and what you are. Being intellectual in some ways means we become numb about those things. We choose to speculate about things rather than contemplate what we are experiencing. That is the true correlation between analytical meditation and daily living situations. If they are correlated and not divorced, whatever takes place, takes place in a wholesome way. However, if they become divorced, if you become too intellectual and pay no attention to your daily situations, there is no intelligence at all. Your intelligence has become severed from your experience and you don't reflect on that at all. This also applies to the other extreme, where we just want to feel and not look at something.

QUESTION: Sometimes I think I have the answer to something and then, as time goes on, I change my mind about what the answer is. I don't trust my analysis any more.

RINPOCHE: Well, that's okay, that's what analytical meditation is all about. If you feel comfortable saying, "Finally, I've done it!" That might be more deceptive than inquisitive. That's what this whole thing generates. You become more and more inquisitive about things. There is no stopping on that level. But, at the same time, if you reflect on the whole thing, you realize you have learned so much through that analysis despite not having gained any definite answers. Everyone wants some definite answer, "This is it!" However, you don't get to that stage. You would feel you have really understood a lot about yourself through the analysis.

A definite answer comes along only when you have obtained some kind of meditative state. You just don't get any kind of real answer, but whatever you learn is an answer in itself. That type of trial and error dialectical procedure is taking place all the time. You commit one error and that is corrected. You make another error and then that is corrected. But it's a hierarchical procedure. Each mistake is more sophisticated than the previous one and the next mistake is more sophisticated than the last one. It's really like that. If you want to be a mathematician, it applies. If you are doing a job, it also applies. If you are doing business, again it applies. You learn more and more. From each mistake, you learn more.

Meditation or the spiritual path is no different. The only difference is that you can't take something and say, "Look what I discovered during my meditation." You can't show it to others; it is not a public phenomenon but that is how it happens. If you look at yourself, you will discover that each mistake has not been a real mistake. In some ways, it has enhanced your intelligence. Because you made that mistake, you are able to look at it from another angle. That's what the path is about. If you have the answer, you don't need to meditate. You don't need to take any journey, because you are already there. A journey involves this dialectical procedure of trial and error but you are becoming more sophisticated all along the way.

QUESTION: Is the outcome of this trial and error process working with traces and dispositions to develop ultimate freedom?

RINPOCHE: Ultimate freedom is being completely free from your own traces and dispositions. That is what the whole thing is all about. However, if you take ultimate freedom to mean you are so free you don't have to conform to anything, it would be a mistake. Freedom really is subjective, and that sort of freedom can be achieved. You would also be more spontaneous and so on because you are not subject to traces and dispositions. You could act one way or another. You have a lot more possibilities. With traces and dispositions, you act the same way again and again. If you are an angry person, you might act quite differently from your usual way for a while, but then it becomes habitual and there is no creativity and spontaneity at all. However, the more you are able to relate to that anger, the more room there is for creativity and spontaneity. That is the expression of freedom.

People complain about external influences all the time, "I am compelled to do this, I am compelled to do that," because of this, that, and the other thing. The whole blame is placed on external circumstances. But no one really bothers to look inside and see how they have been imprisoning themselves through certain acts and the consequences of those acts. If we do that, we begin to discover our external influences are really not so great at all compared to what we are doing to ourselves. It's as simple as that. However, we normally don't want to realize that. It's much easier to say, "These people are responsible," or "This circumstance is responsible for what has happened to me." We do not want to look at ourselves. It's always up to us to make decisions. You could be in one situation or another, you could be doing this or that, and all these possibilities are there. But a lot of the time, even when we want to make these choices, we think we have made a new choice but in the end it turns out we have made the same old choice. We always say, "This time it's going to be different," but it turns out to be the same old story.

QUESTION: Do traces and dispositions exhaust themselves or once created do they remain forever?

RINPOCHE: They get exhausted. You begin to introspect, you develop prajna and consciously create positive traces and dispositions, and then you transcend them. That's how you exhaust them. First you discard the bad traces and dispositions and then you try to replace them with wholesome ones. Then you transcend those until you begin to discover that the substratum of awareness and the rest of it have been quite positive all along. The transmutation takes place here. You don't throw them away as much as discover their own innate nature. Even the negative traces and dispositions have some kind of psychic energy. The practice channels that energy into something more positive. At first it might be a habitual process to a certain degree but in a much more wholesome way. It gradually becomes less and less habitual because you are giving the traces and dispositions less and less chance to rest. Finally you realize that your own substratum of awareness is wisdom, as Buddhists would say. In Christian terms, it may be God. If there is such a thing as God, that is it. You discover your own richness there.

QUESTION: So there is a continual process. You might transcend some of the coarser negative traces, but you still have some subtle ones remaining.

RINPOCHE: In Buddhism, the traces and dispositions are traditionally classified into two levels. The first is emotional instability and the second is intellectual perplexity. Emotions are much grosser and rugged, much more dramatic. You are able to detect them and you begin to become less and less neurotic. Emotions should be understood here as neuroses. Compassion, love, and joy are also there and they could be regarded as emotions too. All the neurotic tendencies begin to diminish, because they are much more dramatic and we can detect them. Intellectual perplexity is mainly related to all kinds of metaphysical questions. You don't have to be a philosopher to have certain ideas about who you are, what you are, and what the world is all about. You might have all kinds of misconceptions due to that and you work through that later on. This is also emotionally charged, mind you, but in a much more subtle and sophisticated sense. This goes on for quite a while, even when you are relatively awake, even when you begin to realize your own substratum of awareness as wisdom or buddhanature. Even the traces and dispositions become more and more sophisticated, so a trial and error process applies there as well because you have more sophisticated errors to deal with. This procedure takes place continuously. But still, in some ways, detecting one error is a step forward. It's not as if you haven't made any progress at all. Sometimes you might feel that way, but still it's a step forward.

QUESTION: One of the greatest disappointments is when some disposition I think I have become aware of disappears for a couple of year and then comes back.

RINPOCHE: You need to have a regular practice. If you practice regularly, you can really work through that. A lot of the time you might feel, "Finally, I have the answer" and you begin to relax and don't do anything until the whole thing hits you on the head again, so that you can't help but wake up, only to realize you haven't really continued with the whole procedure. In some ways, that is the reason we need to have a regular practice.

Five Object-determining Mental Events

We are going to discuss the five object-determining mental events (*yül nge nga*). Here *Yül* means "object," *nge* means "determining" and *nga* means "five." They are called "object-determining" mental events because whenever we have any perception of the physical world, one or more of these mental events will always accompany that perception. They are a necessary component, in some sense, as far as our perception of the world is concerned. The object-determining mental events are interest, conviction, mindfulness, concentration, and prajna.

INTEREST

The first one is known as *dün pa*, "interest." Interest, in this particular context, is distinguished from desire but people normally tend to confuse the two and are unable to make a distinction between desire and interest. They instead think that if you desire something you are taking an interest in it, or if you have some interest in something you desire it. The *Abhidharmasamuccaya* makes a sharp distinction between interest and desire however. It claims that interest is related to appreciating or seeing an object as it is, while desire is related to using a certain object for our own purpose. There is always an end in mind when we desire something, but that is not so as far as interest is concerned. We just take an interest in whatever is presented to us.

We could take an interest in things that are presented, purely through sensory perception, as sensory inputs. We see a particular object and begin to take an interest in it or we hear a certain sound and take interest in that. Interest can be generated through introspection, from observing our mental processes. Interest can also be developed through totally conceptual processes without any sensory input. If someone comes along and talks about a particular person, interest might begin to develop. We might want to meet that person, even though we don't know them. Or if we read about a particular piece of music, interest might develop whereby we go out and buy that record. Interest can be generated either through sensory inputs or through conceptual processes. Nonetheless it doesn't matter which type of interest it may be, it should be distinguished from desire. Taking an interest does not mean desiring something, although interest is at the foundation of desire. Desire might develop later on, but at the stage of interest no desire is present.

CONVICTION

The second object-determining mental event is known as *mö pa* or "conviction." We have to make a distinction between conviction and faith because they are also quite separate. The text says that because we have observed certain events, and seen that certain things have worked in the past, we develop a conviction that they are going to work now. Faith is just accepting something as it is without questioning. Conviction comes from critical inquiry rather than the acceptance of an authority. There is a passage that Buddhist teachers always recite, which roughly translated says, "My teachings are like gold; they should be processed and reprocessed before you accept them. Do not accept my teachings on authority."

Buddha is saying that we should accept his teachings on conviction rather than faith. Conviction is something that develops when you question the teachings again and again. Sometimes, after becoming a Buddhist, we may become doubtful about certain aspects of the teaching and begin to feel guilty. We might say, "That I could doubt such things is impossible." However as far as Buddhist teachings go, that sort of doubt is not regarded as a self-defeating procedure. It is used positively in order to gain conviction rather than to end up as a skeptic. Conviction comes along when we become convinced that something works and we come to recognize that what the teachings say is true.

MINDFULNESS

The third mental event is known as *dren pa* or "mindfulness." Mindfulness as we know is connected with meditation. It refers to the ability to observe our body, speech, and mind. We begin to observe how we behave in those modes: how we behave physically, how we use our verbal ability, and how we use our intellectual acumen. Mindfulness is also associated with past experiences. We begin to see how past experiences influence our present situations and we are able to make some connection between the two.

CONCENTRATION

The fourth object-determining mental event is not something everyone experiences; it has to be cultivated. It's known as *ting ney dzin*, "concentration." We develop the ability to concentrate within the context of meditation. Concentration is not something we can just experience occasionally or experience in terms of our empirical mind. In Tibet especially, people thought meditation or developing concentration was just a matter of concentrating your mind on a particular object or on your breath. However the text says you could meditate upon real physical objects outside of you or on your mental processes. There are four types of object that you can employ as an object of meditation.

The first one is connected with the body. If you are able to concentrate on your body, you are able to see how it behaves and how it operates and so are able to purify your body properly. In other words, you will be able to make a proper assessment of your bodily situations.

The second type is connected with emotions, which are internal. If you are able to concentrate on the emotions and deal with them one by one, you will be able to purify them through the development of concentration.

The third type of meditation is on the Four Brahmaviharas. *Brahmavihara* means "temple of Brahma," but here Brahma doesn't mean the Hindu god, Brahma; it is a psychological term that encompasses four types of mental processes: love, compassion, joy, and equanimity. Love must be distinguished from attachment because they are two different things. We can contemplate on love and we can generate love toward others, but we shouldn't let love degenerate into attachment, because that is a neurotic tendency and can manifest in all kinds of crude or distorted forms of love. Compassion is to be distinguished from sentimentality. If you are compassionate, you could concentrate on that and generate compassion toward others, but if compassion becomes sentimentality the helper begins to suffer as much as the helpee, so that both of you end up becoming neurotic. Compassion is healthy, but it could degenerate into sentimentality, where it begins to manifest as neurotic tendencies. Joy must be distinguished from elation. If you are able to do a few things for others and to begin to benefit others, you might become elated rather than joyful. If you are joyful that is a healthy attitude, but if that degenerates into elation it produces further problems. We are able to properly manage all these processes through equanimity, but equanimity could degenerate into apathy, where you begin to develop the attitude of total hopelessness through feeling that you can't do anything at all. Equanimity is totally different from apathy because it comes from some kind of centeredness or balance. All the other Brahmaviharas can be generated if some kind of balance and centeredness is developed.

This fourth object-determining mental event is totally Buddhist. If you are able to concentrate and study the mind and mental events as they are set out in the Abhidharma texts, those things are regarded as an object of meditation. If we inquire about the mental events, how they operate, what Yogacara or other Buddhist philosophy says about mind and so on, and become inquisitive about those things, they become an object of meditation. Even mental activity can become part of meditation. Meditation doesn't necessarily imply sitting in a formal posture and watching the breath. Meditation can be connected either with a physical reference point or a mental reference point. There is no contradiction between the two.

PRAJNA

The fifth object-determining mental event is again said to be developed through cultivation. It is known as *prajna* (*sherab* in Tibetan). Prajna is "intelligence," but could in some ways be distinguished from the intellect or intellectual processes. Prajna is much more of an inquisitiveness that exists. We might want to explore different things, we might want to study, but these activities are not just for the sake of studying. They are done to clarify confusion and dispel doubts about our existence as well as doubts about the nature of the world. They do not become fruitless exercises but are done as some kind of intelligent pursuit. That is sherab. *Sherab* literally means "best of the intellect." It is to be distinguished from intellectual pursuits of the normal kind, which might be just done for their own sake. Sherab is concerned with clarifying doubts about yourself and doubts about the world. It is concerned with clarifying all those things.

QUESTIONS

QUESTION: How does prajna relate to lodro and rigpa?

RINPOCHE: That's a good question. Rigpa and lodro can both be some kind of ordinary intellectual pursuit. For instance in Buddhism, studying metaphysics or logic might be regarded as the manifestation of sherab. However if you study other things it might just be a mechanical expression of intelligence. You could be a genius, but if your genius is expressed for the sake of being a genius, it does not express your own state of existence. Both lodro and rigpa can manifest like that but sherab is much more than that. It is inquisitiveness about your own existence as well as the existence of the world; it is much more personal. Prajna could develop out of lodro and rigpa. If you are being intelligent, prajna can develop from that intelligence, because prajna is concerned with managing our intelligence in a positive and wholesome way.

QUESTION: I'm not sure I really understand the distinction between joy and elation.

RINPOCHE: Joy is much more persistent than elation but it is also less exciting in some ways. Elation could be emotionally satisfying on a temporary basis, but it is flippant. First you think you have done a fantastic job, and then you begin to doubt it. With joy you feel good because you have generated love, compassion, or whatever. But that doesn't make you feel too elated. There's a sense of well-being. Joy is really a basic sense of well-being. You do whatever you are doing without expecting too much from the other side.

QUESTION: Where does the notion of awareness as opposed to mindfulness fit in?

RINPOCHE: Awareness is connected with sherab, with intelligence, with the fifth object-determining event. In Buddhist meditation we have sitting meditation and we have analytical meditation. Analytical meditation is connected with analyzing the world as well as yourself through understanding Buddhist psychology and philosophy. You begin to question everything. You begin to look into everything. So it is connected with intelligence in some ways. We could say that sherab and awareness are connected, and that awareness is the result of sherab. The more we are able to clarify everything and the more we are able to dispel doubts, the more we will be able to see things in their proper perspective. Through analysis we are able to free ourselves from traces and dispositions so that we see things in their natural state. In mahayana terms it is called *tathata*, which means "thatness" or "things as they are."

To see things as they are means to see things with fewer traces and dispositions so that we are not looking at things in such an ingrained way. Awareness really develops when we are able to see things in their entirety, something that we are normally unable to do. Our perception of the world is quite fragmented. So we first begin to develop concentration where we are able to drag our mind to a particular object. Then awareness develops and we are able to see things within a wider context rather than becoming occupied with certain characteristics of an object and attributing characteristics that are not there to that object. That distortion happens a lot in our perception of things.

QUESTION: In ordinary situations we can be totally absorbed in our thoughts. You concentrate on one thing so much you block out your whole environment. On the other hand you might not be paying attention to what you are doing and that's when you drop something or trip. Is that concentration?

RINPOCHE: Concentration involves some continuity in our perception of the world. Normally when we think about something, or are aware of something, our perception gets intercepted by something else. We are not being mindful so we lose our concentration. Concentration means we are able to direct our attention to a particular object. There is some kind of unity in the way we see things; they are no longer fragmented. Sometimes clumsiness could be outcome of the loss of concentration. Those things are connected in some ways. Traces and dispositions are not totally mental, they are physical as well. To observe how we are behaving and what sort of things are happening, on the physical level as well as on the mental level, would be part of meditation. The more we do that the more insight we gain into our body and mind. We don't have to rely on physiologists and psychologists to tell us how the body and mind work. We could have our own personal insight into the whole thing. In some ways we might know more about our own body and mind than psychologists and physiologists because they are only going to be studying our body from the outside. We are the ones experiencing our body. To make an observation about someone else's body is quite a different thing.

QUESTION: How does concentration differ from mindfulness?

RINPOCHE: Mindfulness is the technique and concentration is the result or outcome of that technique. The more mindful you are the more concentrated you would be.

QUESTION: Should we consider love, compassion, joy, and equanimity to be mental events?

RINPOCHE: Yes, they are mental events, but they are included in one mental event: concentration. You can use them as objects of concentration. An object of meditation doesn't have to be physical, it could also be mental. You could concentrate on love, on compassion, on all the rest, and if you see your love turning into attachment, or your joy turning into elation, that would be meditation in itself. That is developing concentration. Normally you fail to make those distinctions. If you are able to make a proper assessment of those things that would be meditation. You don't need a physical object to concentrate upon; you can concentrate upon your own mental processes, especially the Four Brahmaviharas. Maybe the reason they are called Brahmavihara is because Buddhists wanted to say those things are just as good as the temple of Brahma. There is no explanation other than something like that. First you generate love; you might generate love toward a particular person. Then you concentrate on that love and make a proper assessment of it. If you concentrate on love, some person's image might come up. Any number of things can happen. You have to see whether the love is love or whether it is attachment. You have to make a proper assessment of it. These things would have some bearing on daily life as well.

QUESTION: Is love the opposite of hate?

RINPOCHE: In this particular context love is completely free from attachment so it would be the opposite of hate. However the thing is, if it turns into attachment, it might manifest as all kinds of sadistic and masochistic impulses, which would be more connected with aggression than love. In this context, if you think someone should experience happiness that would be love. If you think sentient beings should be freed from suffering that would be compassion. Joy is just a basic sense of well-being. It has to be contrasted with elation, which means you begin to feel good that you are able to help others or that you are able to do something, and you begin to feel elated about those things. But a feeling of elation brings depression and you swing between the two. With joy you are able to have a basic appreciation of what you are doing, but at the same time, you are not expecting too much out of the other person. You might do whatever you have to do to benefit others so you just accept that. Joy is therefore contrasted with elation. Equanimity would be the antidote to jealousy and hatred. With equanimity you are balanced in your way of looking at the other person. You begin to learn how not to feel aggressive or jealous, you begin to become grounded through concentration and equanimity. That is how equanimity is defined. In Tibetan we say, "Nye ring chag dang, ni den tawa, tang din chimbu." *Nye* means "those who are close to you," *ring* means "those who are far away" (meaning enemies), *chag* means "passion" and *dang* means "aggression." You have passion for the people around you and aggression toward people who are far away from you. *Nyi den tawa* means "free from those two" and *tang din chimbu* means "the great equanimity." The great equanimity is the state where you are free from passion, aggression, and jealousy.

QUESTION: Can you explain how to use these Brahmaviharas?

RINPOCHE: You concentrate on love or on compassion by thinking, "I'm going to concentrate on love" or "I'm going to concentrate on compassion," and you just see what comes into your mind. Then you go on from there and see how you feel about the whole thing. If an image of a particular person comes up, you have to find out how you feel about him or her, how you respond to that. Is your response love or attachment? Is it sentimental or compassionate? What is the case?

QUESTION: Does everyone's conviction have to be the same?

RINPOCHE: Conviction really comes from doing practice and study. You come to have more and more clarity and things begin to fall into place. You just don't jump in and hope for the best, which is a kind of faith. With faith, you just jump in and then you have paranoia about feeling doubt, because you have a basic fear that something might be revealed to you that will repudiate your faith. Conviction is something that comes along in time. Even after you have undertaken a particular practice or study, you might go through all kinds of different opinions. Your conviction grows despite the fact that your opinions are changing. The two are quite different. However opinions could produce conviction. You can't develop conviction without opinions. You do different things and then you begin to see how this works, how that works, how this is true, how that is true, and then you develop conviction.

Eleven Healthy Mental Events

Certain mental events are regarded as healthy and others are seen as unhealthy. Practice is in some sense oriented toward cultivating the healthy mental events and dispensing with the unhealthy ones. According to the Abhidharma eleven mental factors are essential to Buddhist practice and they are actually regarded as quite healthy for the individual. There are eleven healthy mental events. These include confidence-trust, self-respect, decorum, nonattachment, nonhatred, nondelusion, diligence, alertness, concern, equanimity, and nonviolence.

CONFIDENCE-TRUST

The first one is known as *depa*, "confidence" or "trust." Sometimes people translate it as "faith" but we must keep in mind that in Buddhism, faith is not regarded as a premise from which you start and then come to some conclusion. Faith is regarded as a conclusion rather than a premise. You develop "confidence-trust" through your practice and through study, rather than having faith right at the beginning and then getting disappointed or beginning to despair at some other stage. Confidence-trust is divided into three subcategories.

Lucid confidence (*dang bay depa*): this is connected with the notion that we adopt certain procedures for practice and having dealt with that, begin to experience certain things and we gain trust in our own practice. We see the validity of the practice and in some sense the infallibility of the practice. We might make mistakes along the way but the practice becomes more and more valid as we advance. Lucid confidence is something that begins to develop along with our practice.

Trusting confidence (*yid che gyi depa*): this is connected with the notion of karma, because we experience trusting confidence when we begin to see how the law of karma operates as we pay more attention to our daily situations and our practice. Karma is no longer a Buddhist metaphysical concept as we discover how it really operates in everyday life. For example, you buy a shirt and the lady behind the desk makes a mistake in the change in your favor and you feel good and keep quiet and walk out of the shop. However when you get in the car, you realize you have got a parking fine. You pay for your dishonesty sooner or later. This happens constantly. The law of karma is no longer a Buddhist metaphysical principle or just some jargon we use, "It's all karma." It begins to become personal and sometimes too painful that such things are true: karma operates in our everyday life constantly, all the time. So we develop trust in it, obviously. It is really true and so personal. This kind of trust is known as trusting confidence.

Longing confidence (*ngön dö gyi depa*): this is connected with the notion of the Four Noble Truths. First we discover there is suffering in the world. We experience it; otherwise we would not begin to practice. There's this sense of suffering so we question the origin of suffering. We experience that as well and it dawns on us that there is a possibility of terminating this suffering. We discover that such things are actually possible. So in some ways we look forward to the path. From there, confidence begins to develop and we long for experiences we have not yet had. Because the other descriptions of the Four Noble Truths have proven to be right we have the inspiration to journey on. That is why it's called "longing confidence." There is a general sense of trust happening at the same time.

Normally we trust something that brings pleasure or something of that sort but the text says that developing confidence-trust does not necessarily bring any pleasure. We have to make some distinction between the two situations. If something brings about repeated pleasure, we might have trust in that thing, but that is a bit naive. Vasubandhu uses the example of drinking wine; this brings pleasure but it does not necessarily produce trust. We might derive pleasure from looking after our children but we might not actually trust them. We have to make that kind of distinction. Pleasure and the things that produce pleasure may not necessarily be the objects of trust. On the other hand we might trust something but not like it. For instance, the more we meditate, the more we see the validity of meditation. We begin to trust it but we might not really like doing meditation. It is painful but there is some kind of trust that begins to develop through meditation. Nevertheless what we trust does not necessarily bring any kind of pleasure. Sometimes we could actually have both situations—trust as well as pleasure—and sometimes we might not have either. We might not have trust and we might not have any kind of pleasure. These sorts of distinctions are quite important in terms of developing trust. Otherwise we might get these things jumbled up and become confused.

SELF-RESPECT

Through self-respect (*ngo tsa shepa*), we can refrain from engaging in things that are totally disastrous for us. Through self-respect we are able to uphold human dignity and not degenerate to the level of animals. We begin to use our own personal judgment as a criterion for saying what we should and should not get involved in. This sense of self-respect is totally necessary as a healthy component of spiritual practice. Through it we are able to avoid circumstances that are harmful to us and cultivate things that are healthy for us. These things can develop only if we have self-respect to begin with.

DECORUM

The difference between self-respect and decorum (*tsel yö pa*) is the difference between public and private judgment. Decorum is related to public judgment. We do not engage in certain things because people begin to despise us or might feel that what we are doing is detestable. Whatever may be the case, we use other people as the criterion for not engaging in things that are socially unacceptable. So decorum makes us refrain from situations that are harmful toward others. In terms of self-respect we are refraining from things that are harmful to ourselves.

NONATTACHMENT

Nonattachment (*ma chag pa*), as the term implies, is quite simple. In whatever takes place, there is a general sense of the absence of attachment, of not hanging onto things. Things come and go and we are able to let go of them rather than hang onto them obsessively. There is some sense of guardedness.

NONHATRED

Nonhatred (*zhe dang mepa*) is again quite straightforward. Nonhatred does not only mean that we should not continue to feel aggressive but also that we begin to give up any kind of destructive tendencies we have toward ourselves. Any kind of aggression is repudiated. So there is a general sense of the absence of hatred.

NONDELUSION

Nondelusion (*ti mug mepa*) does not particularly mean we become clever; it is just a general sense of wakefulness. We are able to see how karmic situations operate, how karmic law operates, and we begin to realize who we are and what we are. It is a knowledge developed through spiritual practice rather than any kind of technical knowledge that we might possess. Nondelusion is a general sense of understand our practice and our own development.

DILIGENCE

Diligence (*tsön chü*), in this case, does not necessarily mean we begin to be diligent about practical things. It is diligence in terms of persevering with our practice or development. Even when we are confronted with obstacles of all kinds, we do not get disheartened, we persevere. It's said that diligence is associated with things that have to do with wholesomeness rather than anything else. We might be diligent about going out to have our daily bar of chocolate or we might go out just to be in the rain but that is not regarded as diligence. Diligence really means that we are able to persevere with meditation. A lot of people think that as soon as they sit down their mind has to be calm and peaceful. If it is calm they feel good about it, but if they do not experience those things they think there is something wrong with them instead of simply persevering with the situation. Diligence is something of that sort. Obstacles may arise but still we have to persevere. Perseverance is connected with developing oneself. It is said that the definition of *diligence* is "being diligent about upgrading oneself or cultivating what is called wholesome."

ALERTNESS

Alertness (*shin tu jang pa*) is divided into two: alertness of body and alertness of mind. It is the opposite of laziness. We do not just crouch in a corner like a bag of potatoes. Even physically there is some sense of wakefulness taking place, which is called "alertness of the body" (*lü kyi shin jang*). It is said that if we begin to let our body rot, if we really become slack, we have to clean it up. It is the same thing as far as the mind is concerned. Alertness makes our mind much more lucid. It is the opposite of sluggishness. That is called "alertness of mind" (*sem ki shin jang*). Synchronization of body and mind begins to take place so that things are taken care of on a daily situation and we are quite alert.

CONCERN

Concern (*ba gyö*) means something like being an observant or perceptive person. We begin to become quite sensitive toward different situations and toward other people's viewpoints and cease to be too dogmatic about our own viewpoint. We can sympathize with others rather than having to push our own viewpoint down their throats. We are able to be open on that level and also be aware of other people's needs and demands.

EQUANIMITY

Equanimity (*tang nyom*) was discussed previously in relation to meditation as the antidote to elation and depression. Normally we might feel excited about certain things and then if bad news is brought to us, we immediately feel depressed. Equanimity just means we are able to relate to things in a much more stable manner. It is said we could develop equanimity through paying attention to a particular object without viewing that object as beautiful or ugly but just by looking at it as an object. We develop that mental attitude and then extend it into other areas of our life. Equanimity is, in some sense, regarded as the foundation from which we develop all the other positive mental events.

NONVIOLENCE

Nonviolence (*nam par mi tshe*) does not just mean refraining from killing insects or animals; it is also related with not having any kind of aggression. Whatever situation we may be confronted with, we are able to accept it as it is without becoming resentful. We don't look for a scapegoat, we don't blame anything. We just relate to a situation as it is. The cultivation of gentleness and humbleness are associated with this particular mental event.

QUESTIONS

QUESTION: You translated *shin jang* as "alertness." In some shamatha teachings it is translated as "thoroughly processed." Is that the same thing?

RINPOCHE: "Thoroughly processed" is a literal translation where *shin* means "thoroughly" and *jang* means "processed." However it really means "alertness" because you are not so bogged down that you don't know what's going on around you. There is a general sense of wakefulness where you are able to see what's happening. This applies to the body as well as to the mind. We can't meditate by lying on the floor or with our feet up in the air for this reason. Sitting the way we do is regarded as totally human. Animals can do all kinds of things but they can't sit on a cushion like human beings; in some ways, it is as simple as that. With your spine straight and your body placed in a particular posture you feel more dignified and more wakeful. Mind is associated with that as well so your mind begins to become more lucid too. When you are tired, your body becomes heavy, your arms begin to hang, your shoulders droop, and all the rest of it. If you are able to develop alertness of body, you will be able to hold your posture better even in normal circumstances. That would be a sign of the development of alertness of body. Alertness is not purely mental; it is also physical, which is really quite interesting.

QUESTION: Is alertness developed through sitting practice? People who do aerobics and jogging have really good posture.

RINPOCHE: In some ways, that has something to do with it, but the thing is you do not develop alertness with any kind of extreme basis. You develop mental alertness as well as physical alertness. That is a really important point—you just don't develop your physical side; you also develop your mental side.

QUESTION: Is accepting a situation as it is without becoming resentful the end result of processing an aggressive attitude? Is that the final result of one's practice?

RINPOCHE: That's right, sometimes people think that from the moment they are born, the world owes them something. They feel they have come into the world to collect debts. We might not be such an extreme case, but we feel resentful about all kinds of things. Sometimes we might think, "Why should I be in this situation?" We look for scapegoats, for some kind of reason, but we are unable to accept the situation as it is. Nonviolence really means being able to accept the situation. It is not just about refraining from creating painful situations for others; it's also about not producing painful situations for yourself. That's another aspect. Normally when we talk about nonviolence, we are talking about not creating harmful situations for others, we don't think about it in terms of ourselves. But nonviolence applies to ourselves as much as to others. If you are creating harmful situations toward yourself, if you are creating a situation where you are suffering, you are not able to have a nonviolent attitude. If you can't accept the situation you are in, you are creating a difficult situation for yourself, which is related to resentment toward the whole thing. You might begin to resent yourself, you might begin to resent the situation, and you might begin to resent other people. All those things get interrelated. With the nonviolent attitude, you accept the situation you are in, you accept other situations as well, and you accept your own perception of it.

QUESTION: You might feel you've been wronged and you want to strike back, so you put yourself into a situation where you could be attacked. Seeing the situation as it is seems to relate to after you have become involved in a situation.

RINPOCHE: That's right. If you are not involved in the situation, how could you see it as it is? You have to be involved in a particular situation when you begin to look at it properly. The thing is, if you can accept that fact, that's good. That is what facts are. *Fact* means "That is how it is and there is nothing you can do about it." You have to relate to it as being fact. You don't try to change it or expect something else to happen.

QUESTION: What do you mean? If something happens to you, you can let the situation go and just leave it as it is, or you can try and change it?

RINPOCHE: Certain situations are like that but there are other situations that you have absolutely no control over. For instance, if you are born as a white Australian and you resent that fact, there is nothing you can do. You are stuck with it. You are put into that situation and that's a fact. If you are unable to accept it, you are only going to have problems; you are never going to solve anything.

QUESTION: In terms of these eleven mental events, I can't find anything where you can look at a situation and take positive action out of it.

RINPOCHE: They are all oriented toward action, because it's not good enough to have an attitude and not implement it. As far as Buddhists are concerned, your intention and your action have to be coordinated all the time. You can't just have an intention and not implement it or just act arbitrarily without making a proper assessment of your action. Those two things have to go together. All these mental events are both intentional as well as action oriented.

QUESTION: I don't see that as a mental event. To me this is more like developing character.

RINPOCHE: Mental events could be healthy or they could be unhealthy. They are not all oriented toward building character. Maybe the positive mental events are related to making you a better person or helping you to relate to situations in a more positive manner but there are other mental events that are not that way at all. There are unhealthy mental events. *Mental event* really means "any mental process." Mental event does not mean anything dramatic. If you feel like going out to have a cup of coffee, that would be a mental event too.

QUESTION: To me these eleven things are attitudes brought to bear on mental events. I'm having trouble understanding why they are called mental events.

RINPOCHE: An attitude would be a mental event too. That's the thing. An attitude itself would be a mental event. *Event* means "it is taking place in a particular, temporary, duration." That mental process has some kind of temporary duration. That is what "event" implies. You have this mental process that lasts for a certain period of time and you happen to be concerned with it in that given situation. That is what a mental event is. You could regard these things as positive attitudes but positive attitudes themselves would be mental events because when you have adopted an attitude, it takes place in a given context and in a particular, temporary, situation. That attitude would last for a period of time so it is a mental process that occupies a particular, temporary, duration. That is why they are called "mental events."

QUESTION: Is it possible for all these mental events to be brought to bear simultaneously on a particular situation or experience?

RINPOCHE: That is a possibility that we might be able to achieve, but at the beginning I don't think we can have all these mental events taking place at the same time. It's a matter of cultivation. Normally we might be concerned with one thing or another. We might experience more than one mental event at most but we wouldn't experience all of them at once, which really demands a tremendous capacity.

QUESTION: Does every situation have the potential for all the mental attitudes to operate?

RINPOCHE: I think so, because there is a kind of family resemblance, or whatever you want to call it. If you learn how to drive an old, beaten up Holden, you will have a better chance of being able to drive a Mercedes. Once you have learned how to drive, it doesn't matter whether you are driving an automatic or a manual. You are able to relate to those things. In a similar way, if you have developed a particular mental event that happens to be positive you would have a better chance of venturing into the other positive mental events as well, whereas if you haven't really developed any mental event, you would have less chance of getting familiar with all the other ones. All the positive mental events are interrelated. They are not independent of each other. Still you need to get familiar with each one. Realizing one will not necessarily make you realize the others, but if you have realized one it will enhance your understanding of the others.

QUESTION: With decorum is there a danger in trusting too much in what is socially acceptable?

RINPOCHE: Yes, that's why self-respect is mentioned. The Buddhist ethical attitude is quite valid. There is a middle view or middle path expressed here. We can't just go along with everyone else like sheep and follow everything others do. But at the same time we can't become too individualistic and tread on everyone else's toes. There has to be some kind of balance between the two. You uphold your self-respect as well as considering social demands. That's why personal interest and social interest are mentioned. You don't give up your interest just for society and you don't uphold your interest in spite of social interest.

QUESTION: The things that are socially acceptable often seem to be related to illusions of reality. I suppose that's where asserting your own view of reality comes in.

RINPOCHE: Yes, but if you become too individualistic, it doesn't matter how much you pronounce your views, no one is going to listen to you anyway. You will be wasting your breath. However if you are able to adapt to a situation and comply with certain social criterion, what you say is going to have a lot more bearing. This is really practical advice.

QUESTION: Is longing confidence equated with the longing for God in the Christian or Hindu religions?

RINPOCHE: In this particular context, longing is similar to having discovered the two Noble Truths of suffering and the origin of suffering. First, we know that we suffer and then we get into some kind of practice and begin to learn why we suffer. Because we experience that we then see the possibility of terminating that whole process. The path becomes much more of a reality and we long for it. That is what longing confidence really means. We are not longing for something unrealizable. We are longing for something that is realizable so there is some confidence and trust involved in it. That is related with the fourth Noble Truth, in some sense. You are not longing for God, you are longing for the possible experiences you could have. That possible experience is not a fantasy. You realize that since you have experienced the other Noble Truths, the fourth Noble Truth becomes more of a reality rather than a fantasy of some sort. Trust begins to develop in terms of the possible experience you could have.

QUESTION: I'm wondering about nonviolence. In defending my garden I kill snails. What's the karma involved in that?

RINPOCHE: That is a delicate question. Killing snails would have some karmic value but for other killing, it is a really dicey question. From a mahayana point of view, if your intention is totally impeccable there would not be much of a problem. For instance, if someone was going to commit a massacre and you happened to know that and killed that person before they could commit that crime, it would assume a totally different complexion. It is not the same as killing people. So from a mahayana point of view, you could do certain things but you don't do them for selfish reasons. You don't have ulterior motives. With the snails, we cannot say the garden is not more important than the snails. The snails have as much right to live as the garden. What people often do is pick the snails up and take them somewhere else.

QUESTION: Could you please clarify the difference between nonhatred and nonviolence?

RINPOCHE: They are interrelated, but nonhatred is related more to external circumstances while nonviolence is related to both your own situation as well as the situations of other people. It's difficult, because in English they are almost identical, while hatred has a stronger meaning in Tibetan. Inflicting pain on others, taking vengeance, and so on would come under hatred. Hatred would be much more destructive than violence. A Buddhist would say that with hatred you have an intention whereas if you're just wandering around the street getting bored and you knock off a parking meter or put a hole in a road sign, you are being violent arbitrarily. From a karmic point of view, doing something with intention would have much more bearing than just going around doing different violent things arbitrarily.

QUESTION: Disappointment is often connected with hatred or violence. Can self-respect be a counteracting force to keeping on with the hatred?

RINPOCHE: Yes, that's right; self-respect really covers all kinds of ground. It could make you feel more dignified in certain situations because you respect your situation and your own perception of the whole thing and you don't jump up and down because certain things are taking place around you. You don't feel as if you are being undermined by situations and start to despair.

Six Unhealthy Mental Events

We have discussed the positive mental factors necessary for the development of our spiritual practice. We now turn to the unhealthy attitudes and mental events we possess. These are known as the six unhealthy mental events: desire, aggression, arrogance, opinionatedness, jealousy, and ignorance.

DESIRE

Desire *(dö chog)*, in a Buddhist context, means we aspire to something we do not possess. It doesn't matter what it is. We might aspire toward being something we are not. That would be desire. We might want to possess certain material comforts. That would be desire as well. Buddhists would say desire cannot exist if the desire is fulfilled. If we are happy about certain situations there would be no desire. Desire means there is some kind of lack, which is actually intrinsic to human situations. When we realize there is some kind of lack within us we begin to have desire. If we felt good about ourselves or about our material situation, there would be no desire. Desire creates emotional instability. We feel, "If I was such and such a person, I would be so fantastic." That situation does not arise as long as we have desire, because as soon as we begin to attain that particular situation, we want something more.

Desire is therefore intrinsic to human situations. It is regarded as a basic human emotion or a basic unhealthy mental event that we possess. It is said the reason we should not have desire is not because desire in itself is particularly bad but because desire produces frustration. The moment we desire some other situation we begin to experience frustration. That is why desire is regarded as an unhealthy mental event.

AGGRESSION

Aggression (*kong tzo*) really refers to any kind of restlessness we experience. It can manifest in all kinds of situations. It might not be a gross form of aggression—such as wanting to wring your neighbor's neck because he disposed of his garbage in your backyard—it could manifest in a more sophisticated way. Whenever you feel that you have been given the wrong end of the stick, you feel restless and aggressive. There could be a restless mentality that says, "It isn't fair." If we become generous and open with someone and that person turns his back on us we feel that it's not fair. We say, "It's not fair; why has he done this to me?" All kinds of little irritations will begin to manifest. That is really subsumed under the category of aggression.

We might not realize that we are being aggressive. We might think it justified that we feel that way, "This person has not acknowledged my compassion, my sympathy, so I feel betrayed. I am justified in proclaiming my depression. I am justified in proclaiming my despair." But that type of proclamation becomes an expression of aggression. That is the second basic human emotion or unhealthy mental event.

ARROGANCE

Arrogance (*nga gyal*) is where we think we are better than someone else. We come into the world thinking that the world owes us something. We come into the world to collect some kind of debt that is due to us. We come into the world as a tax collector. This kind of arrogance happens constantly. It is a basic arrogance that human beings possess. Seven types of arrogance can manifest according to Yogacara psychology. These are known as basic arrogance, excessive arrogance, the arrogance of arrogance, egoism, the arrogance of showing off, the arrogance of thinking small, and perverted arrogance.

Basic arrogance (*nga gyal*) is about the fact that everyone feels the ego is a necessary component of a human being and this belief has developed into all kinds of psychological and philosophical theories. However it is a basic human instinct, when we are not acknowledged or when we are ignored, to feel our debt has not been paid. We feel that people owe us something but they want to ignore it. This is regarded as the first type of arrogance.

Excessive arrogance *(lhag pay nga gyal)* means that not only do we feel people owe us something, we "begin to lay trips on them," as they say. We begin to encroach on other people's privacy and territory. We express our arrogance in terms of "How could you ignore me? Why can't you acknowledge my existence?" We make a move and set up some kind of strategy in relation to how best to manipulate someone. We take an interest in one or another medium by which we could do that properly so that people will finally realize how fantastic we are. We might try to express it through poetry, through art, and through all kinds of things like that. Since people can't acknowledge our existence, we come up with some trick, some medium, through which we can manipulate another person's sensitivity and we say, "Look at how fantastic I am, look at my ability, look at my intelligence." All kinds of things like that begin to crop up. That is known as excessive arrogance according to Yogacara psychology.

The arrogance of arrogance (*nga gyal le kyang nga gyal*) is where we become totally psychotic. You try to express your arrogance through art or poetry or psychology, but no matter what medium you have chosen, it does not work. You become totally frustrated and go berserk because people cannot relate to what you are trying to express. As a result you begin to become psychotic. Excessive arrogance will then turn into the arrogance of arrogance, which is a further development of the previous one.

Egoism *(nga zo nyam pay nga gyal)* in some ways this form of arrogance is less psychotic than the previous ones. It is really related to the five skandhas. You think, "This is me." If someone says, "Who are you?" you might say, "Well, I'm Jane." If they persist you might say, "I'm what I consist of. What are you talking about?" There is a kind of identification taking place about who we are in relation to our skandhas. There is a basic sense of egoism, which relates to the first kind of arrogance actually. There isn't really very much difference between the two. It might just be that we have much stronger feelings toward the skandhas.

The arrogance of showing off *(ngon pay nga gyel)* is related to some kind of competitiveness. If someone is a good poet or a good musician, we want to prove that we are better. It's quite straightforward. It might also involve some kind of bad taste. Sometimes we exhibit too much of our wealth or ability. We begin to become ostentatious. We try to prove too much. We try to show off so much that the whole thing turns into a big joke. We want to impress others but they are not impressed with us at all. They just see you as having bad taste. They think you have done something but that what you have done is totally off the mark.

The arrogance of thinking small *(chung ze nyam pay gyal)* literally means it is arrogant to think small, which is quite interesting. In the West, being arrogant means thinking that you are so wonderful and fantastic because you happen to possess so many material things or talents. However in Buddhism, even to think that you are small or that you are pathetic is a kind of arrogance. A lot of people actually come across like that. They come up with all kinds of ego mechanisms whereby they express their arrogance through being helpless. "I'm so pathetic. Would you please come and help me? I'm just desperate, I'm so bad." The whole thing becomes another expression of arrogance. To think, "I'm just a speck of dust, I get swayed this way and that way because of other people's influence, I'm nothing," becomes another expression of egocentricity or arrogance. I think a very important aspect of human psychology is being expressed here. As far as Western psychology is concerned arrogance always involves thinking you are terrific. If you do not think you are terrific, you are not egocentric, so they say, "You are fantastic, feel egocentric about yourself." But Buddhists would say if we think we are pathetic, we are still being egocentric, because that is just another means for drawing people's attention to us so that we could live on their sympathy. We nurture our own ego through living on the feedback we receive through other people's sympathy and compassion. Whatever we receive begins to solidify that type of attitude so it is regarded as arrogance as well.

Perverted arrogance (*log pa nga gyal*) does not particularly imply any kind of perversion in the usual sense. It does not mean you have weird sexual preferences or anything like that. Perverted arrogance really involves lack of understanding. We have all kinds of mistaken notions about what we are. We are totally confused so we choose to make up who we are. We form a philosophy about ourselves as to who we are and what we are. It might be totally wrong, totally mistaken, but that particular attitude comes about due to a lack of awareness (*ma rig pa*). *Ma* is a negative prefix and *rig pa* is "awareness," so *ma rig pa* means "lack of awareness." Bad philosophies come about because we do not know what we are. We come up with all kinds of answers as to what we are. We say, "I'm like this because of this, that, and the other thing,' but we have no intrinsic understanding of why it is so, why we are like this, or what we really are. All kinds of mixed feelings and mixed attitudes begin to develop.

OPINIONATEDNESS

The next unhealthy mental event is opinionatedness (*ta wa*), which is divided into five categories: opinionatedness regarding the perishable skandhas, opinionatedness of the extremes, obsession with a particular opinion, obsession with ideologies concerning ethical issues, and wrong or perverted opinion.

Opinionatedness regarding the perishable skandhas (*jig ta*) comes about because we look at our psychophysical constituents or skandhas and feel they are what we consist of, and then we form all kinds of philosophical notions about that. Even though the skandhas may be perishable and mutable, we might think they are not mutable at all or that they are totally mutable and are not going to exist in future lives. We form all kinds of philosophical notions about that particular concept, and that kind of thinking is known as opinionatedness about what is perishable.

Opinionatedness of the extremes (*tar ta*) arises due to the previous notion about the skandhas so that we begin to form the impression that we either exist eternally into the future (the attitude of eternalism) or we perish completely in this life (the nihilistic or materialistic attitude). These two attitudes are regarded are opinionatedness of the extremes. Thinking we are going to live forever is an opinion rather than knowledge of any kind. Plato made a distinction between "opinion" and "knowledge." He said a lot of people confuse the two and think that having an opinion is the same as having knowledge. To equate knowledge with opinion is totally wrong. Knowledge cannot be contradicted by anyone because once you have attained knowledge no one can contradict that. However if you have an opinion, someone can come up with a better one. Your opinion gets undermined because someone else is cleverer than you. But if you have attained knowledge, that is immutable in that sense. In some ways the Buddhist contention is the same thing. If we feel we will live eternally or that we will cease to exist at the time of death, these are both really opinions rather than knowledge, because we do not know. We do not know whether we exist eternally or whether we cease to exist at the time of death. There is no knowledge at all. We might speculate about this sort of thing but speculation involves opinions. Through reasoning, our opinion might be proved to be totally wrong, and we are left suspended in the air from that point of view.

Obsession with a particular opinion (*ta wa chog dzin*) is quite straightforward. To even think your philosophical opinion or viewpoint is superior to someone else's is regarded as totally devastating. You might think being a vegetarian makes your body healthy but another person might think eating steaks three times a day is good. Whatever type of opinion we have, whether it is philosophical or practical, to think it is better than anyone else's is known as obsession with a particular opinion. All kinds of dogmas and political theories develop from this. Communism, fascism, and socialism all developed from this type of opinionatedness. We think our opinion is far better than any other opinion. You might think that Buddhists have the answer so when Hindus talk about *atman*; you want to sacrifice your life to uphold the notion of selflessness. But such a notion is regarded as an obsession with a particular view or opinion.

Obsession with ideologies concerning ethical issues (*tsul trim dang zug chog dzin*). The Jains walk around naked and roll in the dust, sometimes they bark like a dog, sometimes they pierce their tongues and go through all kinds of austere practices, and they might regard that as ethical. Other people might say you should totally uphold some libertine attitude and indulge in all kinds of things. From the Buddhist point of view, these two types of ethical attitudes are kinds of obsession rather than real ethical practices. We might propagate certain ethical issues that relate to sadistic or masochistic attitudes. There are ascetics who destroy their bodies; who poke their eyeballs out and put nails through their tongues. Those actions are not related to ethics because they do not benefit the person or anyone else. They are regarded as an obsession with ideologies concerning ethical issues and not related to ethical issues at all. *Tsul trim* means "ethics" and *dang zug* means "self-torture" or masochistic practices of any kind. In this particular category they are classed as the same.

Wrong or perverted opinion (*log ta*). The *Abhidharmasakosa* gives the examples of *purusa* and *prakti* for "perverted opinions." In a Hindu school known as Samkhya, *purusa* is the "consciousness" aspect and *prakti* is the "material" aspect, and Vasubandhu says that these are wrong views of reality. However any speculation is also regarded as wrong view. As soon as we venture outside of whatever we experience, it begins to become some kind of perverted or wrong view. It is important to realize that Buddhists have never speculated about what happens when one attains nirvana or about the nature of nirvana or what happens to the buddhas after they attain paranirvana. The moment we speculate about such things, that speculation becomes opinion rather than knowledge, because we do not know. So why bother inquiring into those things? It is better to relate to whatever we experience and make a proper assessment of that rather than spending time thinking about what we do not experience.

This is regarded as of paramount importance. To speculate about what we do not experience—about what nirvana is or is not, about how a buddha exists after nirvana, about whether buddhas eat chocolates or have the urge to go to the movies after they have attained enlightenment—is totally ludicrous as far as Buddhists are concerned. In fact all kinds of questions were put to the Buddha about these things and Buddha said he didn't have any answer. Not because he did not know but because to speculate about those things does not help. If you have eaten pizza, but no one else can, to talk about pizza to someone who can never taste it is totally ludicrous. Buddha said these questions would only lead to forming wrong opinions rather than right ones. Speculation can be equated with "wrong opinion" (*log ta*).

JEALOUSY

Jealousy (*tsag dog*) is about having some kind of competitive or restless feeling. If someone possesses something better than you, you want to possess it. This could manifest on the spiritual level as well. When people inquire about what practice you are doing, if it is a practice they are unable to do they might feel they have been left out or that someone is doing better than them. All kinds of things take place on this level. *Tsag dog is* really any kind of competitive feeling; wishing you were better than someone else because you have discovered there is someone else who is better than you.

IGNORANCE

Ignorance (*ti mug* or *avidya*) at this point is really the most important aspect. Ignorance does not particularly mean we are uneducated, that we cannot put two and two together. In fact, if you were to present a complex mathematical formula to a Buddhist master, I'm sure he or she would be baffled. Therefore *ti mug* really means "a basic sense of bewilderment"; it is not knowing our own situation or what we are—we lack understanding about ourselves and other people—so we are unable to make a proper assessment of the whole situation on that level. Ti mug really amounts to not being able to coordinate feeling, intellect, and intuition; not being able to really coordinate between our different capacities of perception. One thing predominates over another so that there is no harmony between our intellect, intuition, and feeling.

Those are the six basic unhealthy emotions. We have gone into a bit more detail about these emotions than the normal presentation. Normally Buddhists just say we should give up ego, desire, opinion, or whatever. In the early Buddhist teachings, Buddha spent a lot of time talking about opinions, saying people should give up their opinions about things.

QUESTIONS

QUESTION: You went into detail about the different aspects of arrogance and opinionatedness but the section on aggression seems surprisingly simple.

RINPOCHE: I did not say very much about aggression because there are no categories there. Aggression can manifest in many different ways, both gross and subtle. It is not simply a case of wanting to kill someone because they happened to stop at a traffic light; aggression can be more sophisticated than that. You could be aggressive toward yourself for instance. When we talk about aggression, we always think in terms of aggression toward someone else but all kinds of aggression manifest in terms of ourselves. A Buddhist would say aggression is obvious so we do not have to say much about it. Desire would be much more subtle so we have to concentrate on its nuances much more. Whenever you feel aggressive, you immediately feel your physical responses and your mental attitude; you can't miss that.

When you feel desire, it's much more subtle, it can take a while to actually realize that it is happening. A lot of the time, you begin to realize what has happened after it has occurred. That's why a Buddhist would say you have to pay more attention to it. It is very easy, especially if you become a Buddhist, to realize aggression but desire exists, even on a spiritual level. You want to achieve something and are never satisfied with whatever you have achieved. When you first start meditating, you might find it very difficult even to sit let alone rest the mind, but once you begin to become comfortable with your physical posture you want to achieve something else. This continues all the time and can manifest in a spiritual as well as a material sense.

QUESTION: Were you saying that wrong or perverted opinion is when you speculate about the nature of things rather than concentrate on discovering the nature of things?

RINPOCHE: Yes, opinions are related to interpretating things, especially in terms of interpreting your speculations. Buddhists may give interpretations but opinions are mostly related with speculating about what might have happened in the realms of things that are totally extrinsic to our experience. What might happen in the state of nirvana? What might happen when someone attains buddhahood? Might you continue to live eternally after death or might you not live after death? To say that you are finished when your body is decomposed would be speculation. How do you know? You don't know. Even a person who is dying would not know, so that would be speculation as well.

QUESTION: Wouldn't the belief that there is a state of nirvana also be speculation?

RINPOCHE: No, because *nirvana* is defined as "the cessation of suffering."

QUESTION: But if you are interested in the path, you have faith that there is a goal, that there is a state of cessation of suffering. It seems to me that this is also speculative because we don't know that; we just hope.

RINPOCHE: No, I think that's different. We don't know what happens after nirvana, but we know what happens up to nirvana. The testimony of people who have attained nirvana bears out the fact that nirvana is possible. Buddhas and the other Buddhist masters have said such things are possible and have given examples as to how it is realizable. It is not in the realm of the possible; it is in the realm of certainty, in some sense. However we cannot speculate about what happens after nirvana. What happens to a buddha when he dies? There is no buddha to tell you what happened. Buddhist masters, after they have passed away, cannot tell you what happens to them. To speculate about that would be totally ridiculous because there is no public testimony to prove whether they still exist or not. You can read the Buddha's original works to see what he had to say about this. He advises us to try to relieve our suffering instead of worrying about whether we will exist eternally. You might end up being neurotic in a future life, so you should try to make sure you do not become so neurotic now, instead of thinking about eternity or annihilation. All those things are really speculative.

"Opinion" is *drsti* in Sanskrit and *ditthi* in Pali. While *samma-ditthi* means "right view." That is part of the Eightfold Noble Path and Buddha spent a lot of time discussing that as well. This is where Buddhism can be distinguished from other religious traditions. For Christians, God created the world out of nothing. You have this world and you have heaven, and when you die you go to heaven and live there eternally if you have managed your affairs properly. If you have not managed them properly you are doomed forever. In most of the Hindu traditions, you possess a soul and live eternally in whatever form you exist. Buddhists would say there is no guarantee of that.

QUESTION: Wouldn't the Hindus also say that is not speculative, it has also been shown by living or previous masters of the Hindu tradition who have attained that state of atman?

RINPOCHE: That's right, but still, what Buddhist masters talk about is what they have realized. Hindu masters might have come to the cessation of suffering, they might enjoy a certain kind of bliss, but they have not shown they can exist for eternity. How have they shown it? They have just talked about it. It may be possible to live eternally but how do we know? Once the Hindu rishi has died there is no one to provide any testimony as to what has taken place. Buddhism lies between strict materialism and strict religious tradition and people should realize this. Buddha never said you could exist eternally even as a buddha. Nor did he say that you stop existing after you have realized samsara is futile.

QUESTION: How do we know a buddha is a buddha?

RINPOCHE: Because he has realized the cessation of samsara. That is the whole point.

QUESTION: But how do we know that?

RINPOCHE: Because we have seen it. A buddha is not just Shakyamuni Buddha. In Hinduism you might talk about Krishna, in Christianity you might talk about Jesus Christ, but in the Buddhist tradition any realized being would be a buddha. Buddha doesn't mean Shakyamuni Buddha; buddha could be anyone. In the Zen tradition, Dogen Zenji—or anyone else for that matter—would be a buddha. The term *buddha* really means "being enlightened" so any enlightened being would be buddha from this point of view. "Buddha" does not refer to a particular being as Krishna or Jesus does. Being Jesus means being a particular person whereas being a buddha does not mean being a certain individual. Shakyamuni Buddha died 2,500 years ago, but what he realized can be realized by anyone. That is the whole point; this is what we are talking about.

QUESTION: But until we realized that ourselves we can have no idea what buddhas have realized.

RINPOCHE: Buddha was a really systematic teacher. He said that at first you don't have to realize anything, just find out whether your life consists of suffering or not. Find that out and then find out where the suffering comes from. How much are other people responsible for it and how much are you responsible for it? Find out the origin of suffering and then you might come to the realization that suffering can end. Only then can you embark on the path; it is a gradual thing. You don't have to speculate about whether Buddha existed or not, or whether enlightened beings exist in this world at the moment. You just find out what you experience, whether you suffer or not. If you realize that you suffer you then find out where the suffering comes from. Once you begin to realize that, you try to find out how the suffering can be stopped.

That was the genius of the Buddha. Buddha never bothered to dangle a carrot in front of us saying, "If you follow me, everything is going to be all right." It is left totally up to us in a very pragmatic way. If we follow a certain procedure it is up to us to realize how those procedures take place.

QUESTION: We desire because we want to acquire something someone else has. However there are many people who appear to be happy because they haven't seen anything better.

RINPOCHE: That is the whole point of the deception we suffer from. That's what deception means: thinking you are happy. But how are you happy? These people are not happy at all. Even here in Australia, there are people who have two cars, a yacht, and can afford to go to Bali every year, but they are not happy. Instead of having a Holden, they want a better car. They want to change the yacht into something bigger. Instead of going to Bali, they want to go somewhere else. Instead of having a particular business enterprise, they want to do something else. All kinds of things come up. Just to think that everything is okay really does not help because desire is still there. *Desire* means "wanting to change from the existing situation to something else." A lot of people do not want to know about spirituality. They are happy the way they are from a spiritual point of view but they are not happy in an overall situation. They still want to constantly improve themselves. The more they achieve the more they want to achieve, so it's a vicious circle. That is what desire means. It is not a desire for spirituality, a desire for spirituality would be much more positive than a material desire.

However once you begin to have a desire for spirituality, you don't really need desire at all, because you already possess buddhanature. You are already rich and wealthy inside so why desire anything? The more you can recognize your own inner wealth, the more you are going to be able to realize it. Nonetheless at the beginning you have to make that journey because you need to break through the deception you suffer from. A lot of people try to be the way they are in all kinds of circumstances. They think they are what they are but they suffer from all kinds of deceptions. You need to have some kind of spiritual aspiration if you want to break through that. Once you embark on that you begin to realize that you do not really need to aspire to anything. This is a realization that only comes after you have been aspiring for spirituality. You recognize that you really don't need to aspire after it because you already possess so much wealth and dignity within you. To try to aspire for something that is much more dignifying is really ludicrous, because if you try to borrow something from outside you, you are going to lose it. As they say, "borrowed money is no money." Spiritual realization really has to come from within. Whatever comes from within, you already possess so the question of aspiration would no longer apply at some stage.

QUESTION: Do desires that are connected with attachment have to be negative?

RINPOCHE: I think so, yes. When we look at attachment and desire, desire would be more positive than attachment. *Attachment* means "hanging onto something and not letting go" whereas *desire* means "aspiring toward something you don't possess." Desire implies a lack that you are trying to redress whereas attachment means you already possess something but don't want to let go of it because you think it's going to be useful. It's like hoarding. You hoard a broken bowl because you think it's going to be useful at some stage. Attachment is really like hoarding material things. That applies on the psychological level also. You just don't want to let go of a situation. Sometimes you realize the situation is not healthy but you still do not want to let go. You hang onto it thinking that some kind of magic might happen, that something is going to dramatically change that whole situation. Desire is directed at something you don't possess. You don't desire something you already possess. You might have attachment toward it but you do not have desire. Desire is about wanting to possess the Chinese antique in someone's shop window. You want to possess all kinds of things you do not have—materially, psychologically, and spiritually. It could be really positive at the beginning but it turn into something totally devastating if it is not managed properly. If it is spiritual desire, then desire is a necessary component at the beginning. How do you look for spirituality if you don't desire to change yourself?

QUESTION: At what point does need become desire?

RINPOCHE: When we begin to become too comfortable our desire becomes even more predominant.

QUESTION: It's a very difficult line to draw isn't it? Do you have a car or do you have a bicycle?

RINPOCHE: You draw the line at how frequently you want to change what you already possess. How soon do you want to get rid of your bicycle? Do you get frustrated by the fact that you can only possess a bicycle as opposed to a car and get neurotic about it? That is desire. You need a bicycle, and probably you need a car too, but if you get frustrated by the fact that you can only possess a bicycle and not a car, that turns into desire. How frequently do you want to change it? That is really the point. A lot of people ask, "What's a healthy attitude toward sex? Where do you draw the line between promiscuity and faithfulness?" You can't jump from one thing to the other without looking so that's where you draw the line. You can't say, "I don't want a bicycle, I want a car," and just get rid of the bicycle and try to get something else. Some kind of mindfulness is necessary even on that level. You see how your mind is functioning, you see where desire really arises, and where need comes to an end.

QUESTION: What I consider a need might be a desire to someone else.

RINPOCHE: I don't think there is any problem there, because

from a Buddhist point of view, that is right. You just need what you can afford; you don't desire what you can't afford. That's where desire comes in. A Buddhist would not say that because you can afford more than someone else, you have desire. If you can afford it, that's okay. But the moment you begin to aspire for something you can't afford and get neurotic about it, this becomes desire. If you can't afford a new couch but get neurotic about wanting to dispose of the couch you have as soon as you can get another one, and get more and more worked up about it, that is desire. It doesn't help; it is psychologically and spiritually frustrating. However you need a couch to sit on; you need a couch to entertain other people. There is nothing wrong with that. The moment you want something better than what you already possess, something better than what you can afford, it becomes desire.

That is why it is said that "desire is totally devastating" and is classified as one of the six basic unhealthy mental events. It gets beyond your needs. If you are better off than other people, you need certain things more. You might have more people to entertain; you might need to do more than others. Those things might be needs rather than desires. However the moment you want to have a better situation than you already possess, that would be desire. If you had only one person coming to visit you, you don't need very much. You only need one chair. But if you have got more people coming around you can't sit them on the floor so you need more chairs or a couch. It's as simple as that.

QUESTION: How does a Buddhist decide whether a certain mental event is healthy or unhealthy?

RINPOCHE: Whatever is destructive to you is unhealthy. Whatever integrates your life is healthy.

QUESTION: In some ways aggression could be seen as healthy. Having an aggressive attitude toward things gives you more strength to conquer them or to achieve some goal or end. One could see that as being positive or healthy.

RINPOCHE: I don't think an aggressive attitude can achieve anything in particular. In the end you get knocked down by someone who is more aggressive than you. It operates on that level. Even on a social level it really operates like that. It is a game that takes place, but you don't achieve anything that way. If you try to push all the time, it's going to be a case of who is pushier than you. In the end you get beaten up.

QUESTION: Could you say the outcome of aggression is that you realize there is some need to relax, which means that you have actually learned something from it?

RINPOCHE: Oh yes, sure, and the same is true for desire. At some stage, you begin to realize it's a vicious circle. It's like playing football. You are achieving something until you get beaten by someone else. That operates on a spiritual level or a social level. You can get to a certain point, and when that point is reached, that's it. You get beaten. You can't continue that way forever. Nonetheless a lot of people who approach it that way think they are achieving something so when they get beaten, the resultant turmoil and despair makes them realize the futility of the whole thing and they fall apart. It operates like that on a social level too. A lot of people finally break up because there is someone who is stronger or more assertive than them and they end up feeling total despair.

QUESTION: But you can't go around being nonaggressive or people will walk all over you.

RINPOCHE: I don't think that is true at all. That's a really Western attitude, which says that if you are not aggressive you get trampled on. If you try to be genuine and honest, you might not receive the same response from people all the time, but gradually people will begin to respond to your attitude. You can't say, "I've been genuine for a week and no one has responded to me, so stuff it, I'm going to break this guy's neck." If you really try to be genuine and honest and sympathetic, people will begin to respond to you that way too, and you will see the value in it. The same applies to acting aggressively. If you act aggressively people might not respond to you immediately either. People might take it; they might try to understand you for a while. However after a while they will begin to strike back and you have to strike them again and the vicious circle begins. If you are genuine and honest, that is really what you are, so you are not trying to influence anyone. Being genuine is not trying to be anything. You are not particularly trying to change anyone else's perception. You are just being honest and genuine in your own way.

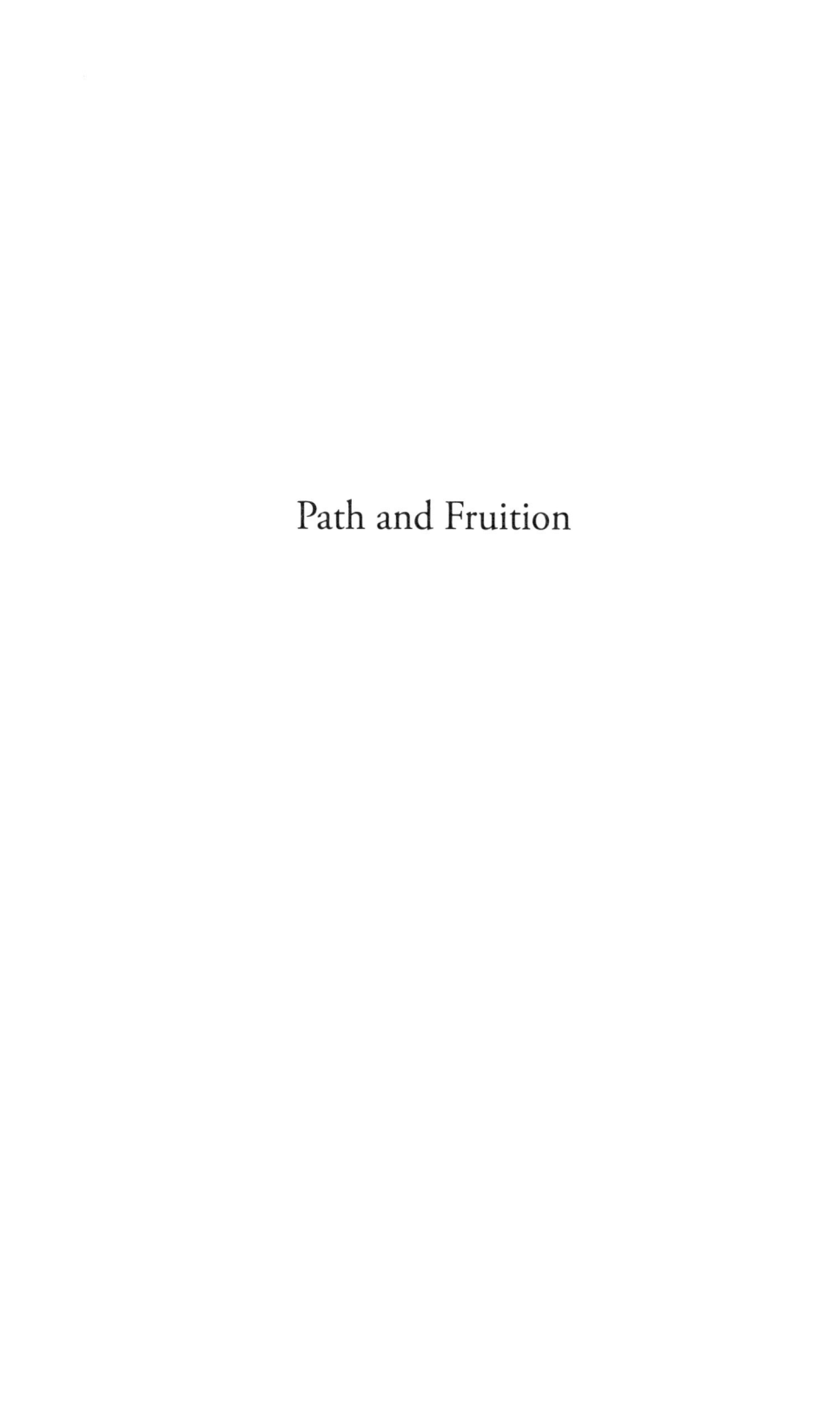

Path and Fruition

Five Paths

We will conclude our discussion by looking at the Buddhist notion of path and fruition within the context of Yogacara philosophy. In Buddhist philosophy generally, the path (*lam*) is divided into five stages: the path of accumulation, the path of application, the path of seeing, the path of meditation, and the path of no more learning.

THE PATH OF ACCUMULATION

In this context the path of accumulation (*tsog lam*) means that after gaining an understanding of Yogacara philosophy, we begin to develop healthy mental events and mental attitudes and concurrently dispense with mental events and attitude that are not conducive to our practice. The path of accumulation has a dual aspect in that accumulation is understood from the perspective of merit as well as knowledge. These are the accumulation of merit (*sonam tsog*) and the accumulation of knowledge (*yeshe tsog*).

The accumulation of merit involves changing our patterns of behavior. For the first time in our lives we begin to see that playing games, deceiving ourselves, telling lies, or whatever it we are doing may be is not conducive to ourselves or anyone else and we begin to modify our behavior. The accumulation of knowledge is intimately related with that. We are able to modify our behavior because we have some intelligence. It is really important to understand this. Unless you have some intelligence, which you develop through practice and through understanding Yogacara philosophy, you might think you are modifying your behavior when you are merely perpetrating another kind of deception. Intelligence is therefore necessary.

These are regarded as the two types of accumulation, which is why this is known as the path of accumulation. This attitude can only come about when we begin to realize how much we are really suffering due to the fact that we continuously deceive and torture ourselves. We might think all kinds of external things contribute to our depression or our emotional instability, but when we look into ourselves, we begin to see we are actually torturing ourselves. So for the first time we treat ourselves properly. We begin to really appreciate who we are and what we are and we begin to make friends with ourselves. This comes about through the two accumulations.

The accumulation of merit is not regarded as an imperative that says, "I should be doing this so I can gain some merit." There is no concept of anything like that at all. The concept of merit is a way to enrich ourselves. It is not so much about what we should or should not be doing and having to suffer conflicts because we have set up all kinds of Buddhist ethical standards. All the merit and knowledge we accumulate becomes conducive toward our becoming wholesome. We become more sane and more satisfied with who we are and what we are, and as a result we stop destroying ourselves. We do not accumulate moral imperatives as such; we accumulate a sophisticated intelligence that is able to deal with situations.

THE PATH OF APPLICATION

This path of application (*sbyor lam*) carries that development further because we begin to apply that whole thing to our daily life situations. *Sbyor lam* means "applying what we have learned through the path of accumulation." We begin to develop confidence in ourselves at this level about how we should implement certain things. We begin to have less uncertainty and also fewer tendencies to regress into our previous lifestyle. That is really the definition of the path of application.

It is said that on the path of accumulation, while we have embarked on the Buddhist path, we might still experience occasional nostalgia. We might think about the good old days and want to rush back to them as soon as possible. We may even manage to do that. However on the path of application that tendency is completely reduced and there would be very little chance of that. Even if we fantasize about going backward it is seen for what it is and remains a fantasy. It does not get actualized anymore. That is known as "not going back" or not regressing. Once we have embarked upon this path of application regression is only a fantasy. It begins to become an evolutionary process in that we cannot help but go forward. We might have the fantasy of going backward but it manifests as a fantasy rather than an actuality or reality. Regression is only seen as a possibility on that level.

THE PATH OF SEEING

At the stage of the path of seeing (*mthong lam*) we see things clearly. For the first time in our lives, we begin to see things as they are instead of seeing things as we want to see them. The path of seeing is intimately related with the ideally absolute. For the first time we begin to see things as they are and that seeing is totally freed from the notional-conceptual and the relative. This means we are totally free from all kinds of wishful thinking, to borrow a psychiatric term. We no longer see things as we want to see them under the influence of the notional-conceptual and the relative.

The notional-conceptual and the relative are intimately related to building up fantasies and fictions of all kinds rather than seeing things in a naked or immediate way. The way we see things is distorted through our emotional and conceptual intermediaries so things are never seen in an immediate fashion. Even when we think we are seeing things immediately they are never immediate. We see things the way we want to see them rather than in a straightforward way. It is said the reason we cannot see things properly is because of the notional-conceptual and the relative, which are related to dualistic fixation.

Dualistic fixation means that we see things in a dualistic way all the time. We do that continuously. We see subject and object, sacred and profane, spiritual and secular, nirvana and samsara, and all the rest of it. As long as we operate on that level, we are operating on the level of the notional-conceptual and the relative, and we will be unable to go beyond that to the ideally absolute. These opposite tendencies create all types of tension and anxiety so that we are unable to ever make a proper assessment of a situation. The whole thing is seen as black and white and clear cut; it is either "this is this" or "this is that." There is no compromise between the two.

The ideally absolute is regarded as a kind of synthesis of opposite tendencies. We can see things clearly when we have a nondualistic attitude. Nondualistic, from this particular point of view, does not mean "numerical identity" such that subject and object are one; it just means that opposites can be reconciled and synthesized so that they become complimentary rather than antagonistic. While we continue to see things in a dualistic way antagonism continues, which creates all kinds of tensions and stains and we are unable to make a proper assessment of reality.

THE PATH OF MEDITATION

The path of meditation (*gom lam*) in this case, does not particularly mean doing formal meditation practice. It refers to a state of ataraxia, as the Greeks call it, a state of "tranquility or serenity." You are no longer disturbed by the opposite forces that operate. You no longer have any type of conflict within yourself as to what you should be and what you are, what you want to do and what you are told to do, or how you want to relate to others and how people expect you to relate to others. All those opposite tendencies get resolved in the form of non-dualism and you begin to become serene on this level.

This is how opposites operate—a fact that is exemplified in biology—where they use the term "symbiosis" to mean that two dissimilar organisms function in such a way they become complimentary. In a similar way all the polarities begin to interact in meditation and this dialectical process begins to break through. A tension that creates another situation where there is a higher level of existence. The Darwinian theory of human evolution says human beings evolved from apes and so humanity included apes in its ancestry. When certain apes started peeling bananas or climbing trees, maybe they did it in a different way to the apes that are still apes. That would have created all kinds of tensions, but the dialectical process between those two species gave rise to human beings. This really operates on all kinds of levels.

Wherever there are two parties that are antagonistic toward each other, it will give rise to a third party. This operates on political, social, religious, and personal levels all the time. If two people are not getting along, there is the very real possibility that a third person will come into the picture, or if two political parties are fighting each other, that might give rise to a third party.

The notional-conceptual and the relative are related with dualistic thinking and dualistic thinking gets resolved on the level of the absolute. However there are different levels to the ideally absolute as well, as we are going to see. On the path of seeing we began to experience some resolution of these opposite tendencies but there is a greater level of reconciliation on this path of meditation.

THE PATH OF NO MORE LEARNING

The path of no more learning (*mi slob pa'i lam*) is where we begin to come very close to being enlightened. There is no longer any question of dualism or nondualism. Even the question of nondualism or reconciling the opposite tendencies that we constantly experience is resolved. The *Abhidharmasamuccaya* expresses this in terms of overcoming two veils: the veil of emotional instability (*kleshavarana*) and the veil of intellectual perplexity (*jnanavarana*). Veil is actually a very good word, because we normally carry these things as masks to hide behind. However we begin to dispense with them on the path.

These two tendencies operate as a dialectical process as well. Normally we feel our emotional tendencies are one thing and our intellectual tendencies are another. We think, "I feel so emotional," or something of that sort but we inevitably come up with some intellectual or philosophical justification for how we are feeling. We have to say, "I'm feeling emotional because someone did this or that to me," or "I feel depressed because of this, that, or the other." We can't just feel emotional without having some kind of intellectual justification for those feelings.

Intellectual perplexity, in this particular case, does not necessarily mean having some kind of philosophical perplexity. I'm sure that is included as well, but even in our basic human experience, emotion and thought cannot really be separated as much as we think. Being human really means having both our thinking and our emotional faculties. These things are intimately related, so the two tendencies operate as a dialectical process.

On the level of no more learning, we have overcome that process completely. Emotional instability and intellectual perplexity are regarded as the ground upon which all the other dualistic fixations operate, and once one has overcome them, all the dualistic propensities begin to dissolve by themselves.

They are no longer a problem. We have gone to the root of the matter, so to speak, once we have overcome those two tendencies. This final stage is called the path of no more learning because once one has overcome those tendencies, there is nothing to learn. You inevitably become a buddha. It is said that buddhanature begins to manifest as buddha's wisdom on the subjective side and the ideally absolute begins to manifest on the objective side. These two get united on the level of a buddha and they cannot be separated. They get united on the ultimate level.

All eight levels of consciousness as well as the mental events that we have been discussing are intimately related with the veils of emotional instability and intellectual perplexity. The dialectical process that takes place between all these kinds of opposite tendencies gets resolved when we embark on the path and progress with our meditation. You begin to come into contact with reality as it is instead of seeing it as a certain thing that might be your own way of seeing it rather than reality in the ultimate sense. We cannot make distinctions in the ultimate sense. Once we begin to attain enlightenment, subject and object can't really be said to be either one or two. We cannot say that they are nondual from the ultimate perspective, because even to say "nondual" is to make another statement. At the same time, they are intimately related. The ideally absolute is intimately related with a buddha's own intelligence, which understands the real nature of phenomena.

QUESTIONS

QUESTION: Do the paths correspond with the ten bodhisattva bhumis?

RINPOCHE: The paths of accumulation and application come before you attain the bodhisattva stages or bhumis. The first bhumi starts on the path of seeing, the eighth bhumi starts the path of meditation and the path of no more learning starts at the tenth bhumi. The eleventh bhumi is buddhahood.

QUESTION: I fail to see why the last path includes conflict, instabilities and intellectual perplexities.

RINPOCHE: You do not suffer from those things on the path of no more learning; you cannot even talk about the nonduality of things any more at that level. Even nonduality becomes a statement of duality in some sense. Nonduality might mean the opposite of duality but that only produces another level of duality. The experiences you might have on that level are free from nonduality, whereas on the path of meditation, you might have the experience of nonduality. You begin to see that opposite tendencies can be reconciled or resolved and you begin to experience well-being and serenity on the path of meditation. On the level of no more learning even that becomes questionable. You can't snuggle into nonduality and feel secure and comfortable. That in itself could become another opposite tendency. It might create the possibility for something else to exist, which is duality. It is not so much a matter of creating something else as creating the possibility of seeing nonduality as something separate from duality.

QUESTION: Is nonduality the same as the Hindu notion of seeing the whole world as one?

RINPOCHE: No, there is a difference, I'm glad you brought that up. Buddhists say *advaya*, which means "nondual," whereas Hindus say *advaita*, which means "one." Hindus would say that *atman* (or soul) and *Brahma* (or reality) are one. Buddhists are talking about *advaya* or "nonduality," which does not mean they are one. Nondual just means that you do not look at things in a polarized way. It does not commit you to any kind of metaphysical stance. It is not saying everything is one metaphysically or that everything comes out of or goes back into a single entity. All the term nonduality implies is that most of the tension and anxiety we experience is due to seeing things in a polarized way. Christian mystics talk about similar things; they see the Godhead as the ground and God as something personal. Godhead is something you partake in because your soul is part of the Godhead. Some people tend to say, "all religions are one," which is a funny thing to say. If all religions are the same why bother to practice anything? That does not mean that all religions are valueless. All religions are necessary but it's good to see the similarities as well as the differences between them. We cannot say what the ultimate attainment is but I think diversity is necessary. Diversity is an expression of progress. The more diversity you have, the more progress there is. When things begin to grow, diversity begins to proliferate.

QUESTION: Are our intellectual perplexity and our emotional instability related or are they separate things?

RINPOCHE: They are intimately related. Sometimes people who sing frantically might say, "I sing songs to God, I dedicate my songs to God" but if you ask them why they are doing so they will come up with some philosophical justification. They really do the singing first but they will have some philosophical or intellectual justification for it in hindsight. They might say, "God has revealed himself to me so it is my duty to sing for him." Those two things are interrelated. A lot of the time we tend to separate those two faculties. We think of emotion as one thing and our conceptual faculty as another thing but that is not true. As long as you are a human being this can never be so. We don't know about chimpanzees and gorillas, but for human beings, thoughts and emotions are intimately related. Sometimes academics and professors get carried away by their intellectual capacities and think they are so ascetic and austere with their intellectual powers that they can dispense with their emotions. That is not so. For example, if you contradict what they say they are going to jump up and down. They want to break your skull. They might stand behind the lectern and lecture and seem cool and austere, but if you start challenging them too much, they will get redder and redder in the face. They are intimately related, which is why Buddhism talks about overcoming those two tendencies.

Normally we are extreme. Either we are too intellectual or too emotional, too obsessed with spiritual things or too obsessed with material things, too obsessed with good or too obsessed with evil. The propensity to go one way or the other is there. However when we go to one extreme the other becomes even more predominant. What we are trying to avoid becomes more predominant and more of a threat to us so the dialectical process continues. We have to come to some kind of reconciliation between those opposite tendencies and this is achieved by understanding the ideally absolute. It is said that all opposite tendencies come about through the veils of emotional instability and intellectual perplexity. They are the ground that creates the possibilities for all the opposite tendencies we develop in our views of things.

QUESTION: After we understand the philosophy, we begin to develop healthy mental attitudes and dispense with unhealthy attitudes which keeps everything moving to the next level.

RINPOCHE: That's the whole point. That's where Buddhist meditation comes in because we begin to see that emotional instability and intellectual perplexity are connected with the mental events and the eight levels of consciousness. We begin to see how that whole thing operates in meditation. We begin to be mindful and to see how we view things from a dualistic point of view, and to see how acting through these dualistic perceptions leaves certain traces and dispositions and makes us even more habituated in the way we relate to things. Our ability to perceive things becomes difficult. That is regarded as the dimming of perception, the dimming of intelligence, because the ability to make a proper assessment of things is lessened and you become more and more alienated from yourself and the world and from reality. You conjure up all these images about yourself and fantasies about the world; a paranoid version of the world where you have no direct contact with anything. You end up dangling in midair, between yourself and the world.

That is why it is called *ma rig pa* or "ignorance." Ignorance does not mean you are not intelligent, in the ordinary sense. You could be so intelligent that you come up with all sorts of tricks to avoid feeling who you are or to avoid coming in direct contact with yourself. You do not want to do that so you come up with all these justifications as to why you are so, why you want to create this new image. When you want to look for who you are, you do not look inside, you look for other things. You look at others and you try to find out who you are from them. You use other people as the criterion to find yourself. That is impossible but that is what people do; they try to find out who they are by looking at others.

QUESTION: Is awareness of what you are doing a prerequisite for embarking on the path?

RINPOCHE: If you want to make a journey overseas first you have to equip yourself with the necessary things. You have to have enough money and make preparations. Once you have done that you get to the next step, which is taking the real journey. Once you are on the airplane, whether you like it or not, you are going and it is hard to come back. It is like that with the path of application. There is the possibility that the pilot might receive a message of an emergency and decide to turn back but that is only a remote possibility. Ninety-nine percent of the time, you are there in the airplane and you are going to get to wherever you are going. In a similar kind of way, once you get to the level of application you are already on the path and regression is only a remote possibility.

QUESTION: It seems that many people are accumulating merit without being aware of it. Is it important to be conscious of following a path?

RINPOCHE: To a certain degree, that is important, because a lot of well-meaning people who do good things for others turn into fanatics. From a Buddhist point of view, any fanaticism is regarded as totally nondharmic; it is not regarded as a

Buddhist way of life. You cannot be fanatical in the name of the buddhadharma. If you embark on a particular path and do certain practices, you are constantly reminded of the fact that you can't turn into a fanatic, you can't become too dogmatic about the whole thing. In Buddhism, the dissolution of opposite tendencies is very important. Getting obsessed with religious or spiritual questions would be regarded as an obsession. It would be an impediment rather than anything else. Otherwise people might think, "That's good; I'm going to change the world with my spiritually."

QUESTION: It requires a conscious effort to develop positive mental events. Is there is any danger there of thinking this will keep you on the path?

RINPOCHE: Sometimes Buddhists try to develop all these positive mental events and they end up driving themselves into the ground because they see how many other things are going on and begin to hate themselves. The mental events are supposed to cool you down, not make you neurotic about the whole thing. When you feel like kicking yourself because you have not been able to develop enough healthy mental events you should think, "This is not right; it means I haven't really adopted a healthy attitude at all."

QUESTION: How should one view an unhealthy mental event?

RINPOCHE: Some Buddhists think, "I feel so aggressive, I should keep the aggression out." However the moment you begin to do that you have adopted an aggressive standpoint. You are so hyped up and pissed off with your aggression; you can't stand it anymore, which is another form of aggression. The basic thing is to just see it as aggression. There is nothing wrong with it. It's part of the human situation. On top of that, you begin to acknowledge that you are feeling aggressive, and instead of expressing it blindly, you feel the energy of aggression properly. You see how you feel when you become aggressive and you gradually try to accommodate that. Aggression can be accommodated. Once you begin to accommodate your aggression properly your need to act out aggressively will lessen.

QUESTION: Does aggression become a positive mental event?

RINPOCHE: Aggression wouldn't particularly get transformed into anything on this level. On the Buddhist tantric level, it is a different matter, but on the Yogacara level it won't necessarily get transformed into anything. You could develop the mental attitude of love and compassion toward your own aggression. In fact you are really beginning to make friends with yourself. You are beginning to appreciate yourself, in some sense, if you can make friends with your aggression. That does not mean you have to propagate aggression; that would not be making friends with your aggression. If you can make friends with your aggression without having an ulterior motive, that is what should be happening. You do not use the healthy mental events to counterattack but to diffuse the other unhealthy mental events. That's what the whole thing is all about. It is not about trying to destroy them. Some people think, "I should be destroying my anger, I should really be destroying my desire," but they end up becoming even more neurotic about the whole thing, because it doesn't happen that way. That whole attitude is negative anyway. Wanting to destroy your anger is a negative attitude to begin with.

You accommodate those things as part of yourself and relate to them as they are. That might not be easy; it is not regarded as an easy step to take. Nonetheless it will have a much more valuable effect in the long run. You can ignore your anger or you can suppress your anger, but in either case that anger is going to manifest in some other form. It is not just going to disappear. The best thing to do is to try to make friends with your anger. Then you are making friends with yourself at the same time. Sometimes we feel angry and destructive toward others, but haven't looked at how we are destructive toward ourselves, how we get angry at ourselves and hate ourselves.

Sometimes people are so nice to others. They don't show any anger but inside they are destroying themselves. People think they are so good, they are fantastic, but inside they are just tearing themselves apart: right, left, and center. You could exhibit all these religious tendencies, but still you haven't really dealt with your anger properly and you haven't really accepted yourself properly. You might be so obsessed with the notion of pleasing others that you are never satisfied with how much you are doing. You just keep saying, "I'm not doing enough, I'm not benefiting others enough, I'm not pleasing them enough." It is only when we begin to accept our own anger that we will be able to be really satisfied with ourselves. We will also be able to benefit others much better too because we no longer suffer from any conflicts within ourselves.

QUESTION: If you deal with your anger in that way, does that mean it dissolves or are you just able to put it to positive use?

RINPOCHE: It would be good to get into how Buddhist tantra views these negative energies. Normally we should stop regarding anger as bad. That is just another way of looking at anger from a habitual point of view. We should regard anger as some kind of energy. It is not necessarily bad or good. Anger becomes bad when it's exhibited toward others or used to destroy ourselves. Anger itself is not good or bad; it is just a kind of emotional energy that we possess, just like desire and jealousy. They are also a form of energy. That's the whole point. Once we begin to have a healthy attitude toward anger, we begin to see the possibility of using that energy in a much more satisfying way. We begin to see that point of view. We can see that point of view only after we have adopted the mahayana perspective.

The transmutation of aggressive energy into something more positive—into something that is not necessarily the opposite of negative energy particularly, but a much more encompassing reality than that—only comes about on the tantric level. However some kind of ground has to be laid where we first learn to accept anger. If we can't accept anger as part of ourselves and develop some kind of friendly attitude toward it, transmutation would be really difficult. We might want to transmute anger because we hate it so much but that attitude does not help. It will just set up another vicious circle, which is precisely what samsara is all about; we go round and round without getting anywhere.

The starting point is to regard anger as some kind of energy that manifests in all kinds of ways. We should accept it as part of ourselves and just see it that way, because the more we disassociate from our neuroses or emotional instabilities, the more they become a problem. That's really true. When we can accommodate our own neuroses and emotional instabilities, we can accommodate all parts of ourselves without having to reject them. To reject our anger would be to reject a part of ourselves. A lot of people think, "If you make friends with your anger, you are going to be so aggressive." But we are aggressive already. The thing is to really find out whether this approach works or not. Either we are developing ourselves or we are being aggressive toward others anyway, so it doesn't make much difference. It is worth trying. It is worth experimenting to see whether it works or not.

QUESTION: Is ego the source of all anger?

RINPOCHE: It all comes from not being able to see ourselves properly. We might talk about ego but we really have no notion of what the ego is. We don't even know what we want to be. Sometimes we have this idealized notion of ourselves, this gigantic version of ego, and sometimes we just feel so insecure and insignificant, which is some pathetic version of ego. There is no real or solid thing to hang onto. We are unable to see ourselves properly because we don't look inside to find out who we are. Our notion of ego has been built up by using other people as our criterion.

Both self-hatred and our idealized versions of ourselves come about from regarding other people as the criterion.

We want to be like someone else, and at the same time, we hate ourselves because we are not like someone else. That is why it is said, "samsara is never-ending." Unless we are totally neurotic or psychotic, we sometimes achieve our idealized version of self. If you want to be a really good painter and get obsessed with that and use someone else as the criterion, you might become a good painter and become famous. But then you want to idealize yourself again. You want to look for something else, use someone else as the criterion. It is a never-ending process because you haven't really accepted yourself. That's why a lot of famous painters and musicians fall apart. Whatever they are trying to achieve turns out to be fantasy and they have come no closer to themselves. There are others who haven't achieved very much at all on the external side but they are really happy with themselves. They are not aspiring to be something that they cannot be. I'm not saying we shouldn't aspire to be anything but a lot of the time our idealized version of ourselves can get out of hand so that it can only be achieved in fantasy or dream.

E-Vam Institute

E-Vam Buddhist Institute of New York seeks to foster the study and practice of the Kagyu and Nyingma lineages of Tibetan Buddhism in the west. E-Vam Institute works to promote understanding between the Buddhist traditions and the other major faith traditions in the world as well as bring greater understanding between the various Buddhist schools and lineages themselves.

E-Vam Buddhist Institute
171 Water Street
Chatham, NY 12037
Phone: 518-392-6900
Web: www.evam.org

Kagyu E-Vam Buddhist Institute
673 Lygon Street
Carlton North, Vic, 3054, Australia
Phone: +61-3-9387-0422
Web: www.evaminstitute.org

Nyima Tashi Kagyu Buddhist Centre
30b Pollen Street
Ponsonby, Auckland, 1021, NZ
Phone: +64-9-376-6113
E-mail: nyimatashi.nz@gmail.com

Yeshe Nyima
49-51 High Street
Harris Park, NSW 2150
Phone: +61-2-9893-9008
E-mail: yeshenyimansw@gmail.com

Books by Traleg Kyabgon

The Four Dharmas of Gampopa (KTD Publications, USA, 2013)

The Ninth Karmapa, Wangchuk Dorje's Ocean of Certainty (KTD Publications, USA, 2011)

The Influence of Yogacara on Mahamudra (KTD Publications, USA, 2010)

The Practice of Lojong: Cultivating Compassion through Training the Mind (Shambhala Publications, USA, 2007)

Nyima Tashi: The Songs and Instructions of the First Traleg Kyabgön Rinpoche, translated by Lama Yeshe Gyamtso (KTD Publications, USA, 2006)

Mind at Ease: Self-Liberation Through Mahamudra Meditation (Shambhala Publications, USA, 2004)

Luminous Bliss: Self-realization through Meditation (Lothian Books, Aus, 2003)

Benevolent Mind: A Manual in Mind Training (Zhyisil Chokyi Ghatsal Trust Publications, New Zealand, 2003)

Essence of Buddhism: An Introduction to Its Philosophy and Practice (Shambhala Publications, USA, 2001)

The Ninth Traleg Kyabgon Rinpoche with the His Holiness the Seventeenth Gyalwang Karmapa, Ogyen Trinley Dorje, at Gyuto Monastery, Dharamsala, India, 2010

A Prayer for Traleg Kyabgon Rinpoche's Swift Return

Primordial, manifest perfection as self-existent luminosity
Ground and fruition inseparable; glorious Vajradhara:
Your form manifests as a wheel of myriad emanations.

I pray at your feet, glorious guru.

Through your oceanic outer, inner, and secret lives
You reveal the face of coemergent timeless awareness
In the mirror of limitless wanderers' minds.

I pray that you swiftly return, glorious, sublime guru.

For as long as samsara has not come to its final end,
May I ever remain your dear disciple and be cared for
By virtue of your tireless compassion.

May I realize the original protector—the state of unity.

At the request of the most venerable and incomparably kind Thrangu Rinpoche and Khenpo Karthar, this prayer for the swift return of Traleg Kyabgon of Ga was composed by Karmapa Ogyen Trinley Dorje on August 1st, 2012.

May all beings be happy!